AFFORDABLE PORTABLES

Revised & Expanded Edition

A WORKING BOOK OF INITIATIVE ACTIVITIES

& PROBLEM SOLVING ELEMENTS

by

CHRIS CAVERT, MS & FRIENDS

Published by:

Wood 'N' Barnes Publishing & Distribution
2717 NW 50th
Oklahoma City, OK 73112
(405) 942-6812 · (800) 678-0621

This publication is sold with the understanding that the publisher is not engaged in rendering psychological, medical or other professional services.

Cover Art by Chris Cavert.
Activity Diagrams by Chris Cavert & Susana Acosta.
Copyediting & Design by Ramona Cunningham.

Printed in the United States of America
Oklahoma City, Oklahoma
ISBN # 1-885473-40-0

MY THANKS

Grand thanks goes to Tom Leahy of Leahy & Associates
for encouraging me to do a pre-conference at his
National Challenge Course Practitioner's Symposium.
It gave me a deadline with which to work.
He also let me use his creative title for all this stuff.
Thanks, my friend.

And of course
Thanks to all the Experiential Educators
who let me share their wonderful ideas with you.

Karl Rohnke
Sam Sikes
Tom Leahy
Jim Cain
Tom Smith
Frank Harris
Brian Brolin
Craig Dobkin
Jackie Gerstein
Lenny Diamond
Madeline Constantine
Clifford E, Knapp
Scott Trent
Earl LaBlanc
Clay Fiske
Lori Armstrong

**Thank you so much, my friends.
Your generosity will touch the lives of many!**

TOGETHER WE WILL MAKE A DIFFERENCE!

CHRIS CAVERT has been a teacher for over 20 years. He has worked with youth and adult groups of all ages. Chris holds a Physical Education teaching degree from the University of Wisconsin-LaCrosse, and a Masters degree in Experiential Education from the University of Minnesota at Mankato. Some of his first writing was published in the best selling *Chicken Soup for the Soul* series by Jack Canfield and Mark Victor Hansen, and his activities have been published in books by Karl Rohnke, Jim Cain and Berry Jolliff.

Chris' other titles include:

GAMES (& OTHER STUFF) FOR GROUP · BOOK 1 · Activities to Initiate Group Discussion

GAMES (& OTHER STUFF) FOR GROUP · BOOK 2 · More Activities to Initiate Group Discussion

GAMES (& OTHER STUFF) FOR TEACHERS · Classroom Activities that Promote Pro-Social Learning (with Laurie Frank)

EAGER CURRICULUM: Experiential Activities, Games & Educational Recreation

WHAT WOULD IT BE LIKE...1001 Anytime Questions for Anysize Answers

50 WAYS TO USE YOUR NOODLE: Loads of Land Games with Foam Noodle Toys (co-authored with Sam Sikes)

RICOCHET & OTHER GAMES WITH AN ODD BALL

Check out Chris' website at www.fundoing.com for more information and fun.

CONTENTS

You have just picked up (lifted off the table; purchased for your own library; met at a bar) Affordable Portables - Revised. So what's it all about, what are you getting for your money?

Affordable Portables is a book of initiative activities and problem-solving elements that you can create and use to start your own experiential challenge program or enhance the program you already have for people 12 and older. All of the ideas here are presented with a tight budget in mind. (The definition of tight will surely vary. If you are unable to afford the price of this book, then you have a "very" tight budget. If you can utilize equipment you have lying around, can scrape up about $500.00, and have access to the necessary tools, you will have one of the most diverse, interchangeable, portable programs available today.)

I do not claim to have created all of the activities here. Many helpful contributions have been made to make this book possible. Some valuable activities have been around "since time began" and some are fresh off the drawing board. Some add wonderful history to the field of experiential education, some could possibly make history.

My purpose? It is to provide a way for human services providers to afford the benefits challenge programming can offer. I believe experiential education and challenge programming can be one of the most effective pro-social development tools available today, when used appropriately.

If you are new to the field of adventure programming, it will take some time, or experience, to find your style. This should be expected. To assist you in your travels I have provided "sparking" questions for each activity and space to add your own ideas along the way. I would hope you will make this "your" book. Your ideas with mine, and all my contributing friends, will create another way to look at the world and all its wonder - if not, at least add some "excitement to an otherwise dull day" (what movie?).

Some thoughts on **how to use this book.** Please do not use Affordable Portables without additional information on experiential education and how it is used with groups. This book is an activity supplement for experiential facilitators. It does not take the place of proper experiential facilitation training. **Improper use of this information could result in injury.** There are some excellent resources available that can give you a good start on the "process." I also suggest that you seek out a qualified company to guide you through the instructional tips and safety of the activities provided here. There is a listing of Experiential/Adventure Based Training Companies in the Appendix section.

Adventure is just that - adventure. Look this word up and find out what it means to you. Enjoy!

> "...the wise leader does not push to make things happen, but allows process to unfold on its own. The leader teaches by example rather than by lecturing others on how they ought to be. The leader knows that constant interventions will block the group's process. The leader does not insist that things come out a certain way."
>
> *John Heider*

This quote from, "The Tao of Leadership," suggests that the leader, or facilitator, "guides" a group through a process - through the group's own discovery of new experiences. From these new experiences, participants can learn how to relate new skills, ideas, and behaviors to future life situations.

Peter Senge, in his book, "The Fifth Discipline," tells us that another function of a facilitator is to help "people maintain ownership of the process and the outcomes..." (p. 246). In this way the group is responsible for their own success and failure; for their own esteem and learning.

So what is the process? Johnson & Johnson define a process as "an identifiable sequence of events taking place over time" (p. 202). This process is carefully observed by a facilitator. This facilitator then is often responsible for initiating "group processing." Group processing "may be defined as reflecting on a group session to (1) describe what member actions were helpful and unhelpful, and (2) make decisions about what actions to continue or change" (p. 203).

Experiential educators deal with process constantly. This is what separates experiential education from recreational participation in activities. So, it would be important to study and practice the skills of processing, or what many call "facilitation." It is not my intention to share my ideas about facilitation within this book. But I would like to guide you to some helpful resources and common practices that have been proven successful.

Some practices include the Adventure Wave Plan, outlined in "Islands of Healing" by Schoel, Prouty, & Radcliff (1988) and the Experiential Learning Cycle in "Processing the Adventure Experience" by Nadler & Luckner (1992). Another common approach to facilitation is, Experience...What?, So What?, and Now What?

Proper ground work is important for the "Experience." First you will want to choose an activity that suits the objective of your session. It should be appropriate for the ability and age of the group, and fit within the limitations of your program facilities. Next, you will want to give clear instructions and safety guidelines, then provide ample time for questions before the activity starts. As the group begins, you become the watchful facilitator; keeping the activity safe at all times.

"What?" happens is up to the group. Some facilitators choose to ask questions about what is happening during the activity. Other facilitators wait until the end to ask. Some facilitators ask during and after an activity. This choice is ultimately up to the style that is most comfortable to you.

"So what?" were you feeling or experiencing during the activity, is next. This is where skills, behaviors, emotions, and feedback are encouraged. Keeping the discussions safe for all individuals will increase the bonding potential of the group and develop the trust levels needed to take future risks. (I would like to suggest that you look into Senge's information on discussion and dialogue in "The Fifth Discipline." This information has helped me to really uncover the "So What?" stage.)

To complete the cycle, "Now What?" are you going to do with any new information that you have obtained? This stage pushes learning into the next activity and, with hope, into real life situations. Making the learning relevant to future activities and life situations is where behavior change starts.

I find the hardest part of the experiential process is not giving out solutions to problems. As adults, it is easy to tell someone how to do something, especially if we have a solution. However, more knowledge is gained by self discovery than lecture. Let the group discover what is in the treasure chest, you can provide the key with thoughtful questions.

Preparation, facilitation, and processing are skills enhanced through time. If you are not satisfied with the way you approached a particular problem, use this situation as a learning "Experience" for yourself; "What" happened? "So What" did you learn from it? "Now What" are you going to do next time? The process is not just for the group. This is what experiential education is all about; there is always something to learn.

As I reflected on my learning experiences around facilitation, the most challenging task became asking the right questions. It was often futile to go into a program or specific activity with a list of questions because often times the group took a direction on the activity that I did not expect. However, I ended up, over the years, with some general questions that served many different situations. I have included some of these questions along with each activity in this book. Please remember that these questions are guides to your learning. Developing your own questions will be the key to your style. (In most cases there is space provided within each activity description to write down questions that were most helpful to you.)

I encourage you to obtain more information about facilitation and processing. Several excellent books and training programs are listed in the Reference section and in the Appendix. A good teacher is also a good learner. Now on to the Adventure!

SECTION ONE

initiative games

THOUGHTS · NOTES · REVELATIONS

If you were to ask an experiential facilitator to list the top five most important things to know about adventure programming, nine out of ten will have "proper sequencing" on their list. Rohnke & Butler (1995) believe, "sequencing is a key skill because the flow of the Adventure experience greatly impacts its success for the participants." Schoel, Prouty, and Radcliffe (1988) suggest the following sequence progression which they plug into their Adventure Wave: Ice Breaker/Acquaintance Activities, De-Inhibitizer Activities, Trust and Empathy Activities, Communication Activities, Decision-Making/Problem-Solving Activities, Social Responsibility Activities, and Personal Responsibility Activities. Almost all of the Initiative Games (as well as the Initiative Elements) in this book fit within the Communication, Decision-Making/Problem-Solving, and Social Responsibility activity areas (I had to add some "just plain fun ones" too). This is why, as I stated earlier, it is so important to understand the full scope of experiential education before diving into the adventure. Find out more about Ice Breakers, and De-Inhibitizer activities, as well as the Trust sequence. It will help you to understand sequencing and why it is so valuable.

Each game within this section will require a small or large group's combined physical and/or mental effort to arrive at a solution to a presented problem. As Rohnke (1989) puts it, "This problem-oriented approach to learning can be useful in developing each individual's awareness of decision-making, leadership, and the obligations and strengths of each member within a group."

Learning? So what is this about learning? Here is where the real "meat and potatoes" begin. After you have initiated and traveled through the process of social introduction, group interaction, and trust building, the time will come to implement deliberate pro-social development.

At this stage of the game, you will wear your "Facilitator's" cap. As I mentioned before, your job as a facilitator is a complex one and requires practice and training. The art of observation and processing are the valuable tools of facilitation. You will learn how to plan objectives, what to notice, and then to ask appropriate questions to <u>bring out</u> the learning from the group. A facilitator will also learn not to tell the group what they have learned but will ask the group.

To assist you in this learning process, I have added a section within each activity on "Observations & Questions." This will help you to choose appropriate goal related activities and direct your attention to common issues and behaviors during each. These observations and questions are based on my past experience with the games and certainly do not represent an exhaustive list. So many different things can happen. It is up to you, as the facilitator, to help the players in the group reflect on their experience.

Based on the intended brevity of this working-book, I have not included a great deal of instructional philosophy. For more knowledge in this area check the references and additional resources in the back. There is more than enough there to keep you reading for a long time.

BIRTHDAY ROPE

NEEDS: You'll want a nice, big activity rope for this one - large enough for your whole group to stand on. (I like old climbing rope the best.)

PROCEDURE: Set the rope out on the ground in a large circle shape. Ask all your participants to stand with at least one foot on the rope. Now, without talking, line up in birthday order - by month and day only. During the moving process, players must have at least one foot on the rope at all times. Ask the players to look at you when they believe they are finished. Check out the order. If there are any errors, give the group time to fix them - without talking.

I'll open up my programs with this activity right off the bat. This is a good one to get people close to each other, and it also provides a taste of what problem-solving is. After checking the correct birthday order, I'll go around with introductions, then talk about what's going to happen for the day.

OBSERVATIONS/QUESTIONS:
- How many of you believed you followed directions?
- What makes it hard to follow directions?
- What was difficult about this activity?
- What type of helping went on? (if any)
- How did you communicate with your group members?
- Did you learn anything from this new form of communication?
- What part did the rope play in the activity?
- Why are boundaries important, and how will they affect our day?
- What sort of problems did we have to solve?
- What sorts of problems do we have to solve on a daily basis?
- Did you learn anything about any of your group members?

(other) •

•

VARIATIONS:
- You can choose any other order line up: Tallest to shortest; oldest to youngest; alphabetical order; shoe size.

ADDITIONAL IDEAS:

9

NEEDS: The number of objects you use within each set will be determined by the number of participants - the more participants, the more objects. You'll need two sets of objects for this one. (Two in each set is good for a group of 12. Four in each set will be good for a group of 24.) Each set must have identical objects in them, either by color or size. I'll use tennis balls and deck rings for the example. The important factor is an even number of players. If there is an odd number, I will jump in and play.

PROCEDURE: Choose a player to start, and hand that person a tennis ball. The starter will hand off the ball to the player two over to her right after saying, "WATCH IT" (with some gusto) to the player directly to her right. The directly right person should duck to avoid the overhead <u>hand-off</u> (not a pass). This same action goes around the circle until the ball returns to the starter - then they hold the ball. Now, that directly right person we talked about, given a deck ring, says, "WATCH IT" to the "next directly right" person who ducks to avoid the overhead hand-off (not a pass). This action goes around to the start. (Half the group passes around the tennis ball, the other half the deck ring.)

Now for the fun. Start the tennis ball, let it get two players down, then start the ring. You'll see how the mental and the physical work together (or not together - I'm still ducking when I'm suppose to be passing - crazy). Add in more tennis balls and rings for some real warm-ups. Don't forget - STOP WHILE IT'S STILL FUN.

I never really spend too much time processing this one. I've mainly used it to warm-up the minds and bodies. However, there have always been interesting things to talk about.

OBSERVATIONS/QUESTIONS:
- When was the activity easy?
- When did it get harder?
- How many things do you think you can handle at once?
- How many things do you think the group can handle at once?
- What are things? What sort of things do you think will be happening during our time together?

(other) •

•

VARIATIONS:
 • Pass the Pasta. This one comes from "50 Ways to Use Your Noodle," by Cavert & Sikes. Cut those long, foam noodle pool toys in half. You'll need two sets of different colors. Following the procedure above, the group bends over a bit and passes across the lower part of the legs and gives the person two players down a nice WHACK.

 I had a large group try both versions at the same time. I started the balls on one side of the circle and the noodles on the other. What fun!!

ADDITIONAL **I**DEAS:

NEEDS: 1 flying disc and a 20 yard span to cross.

PROCEDURE: Using a flying disc, have each individual in the group touch the side of the disc with one finger, without touching anyone else in the group (hair doesn't count as a touch for this one). From this point, have the group move together, about 20 yards, without dropping the disc or touching one another.

OBSERVATIONS/**Q**UESTIONS:
- Was anyone uncomfortable? Was anyone left out? Why?
- Could you add more people? How many?
- Did anyone touch another person and not speak up?
- Who is responsible for following guidelines?
- What was the reaction to dropping the disc?
- Were you able to get past the problems you encountered?

(other) •

•

VARIATION:
- Carry a bucket of water overhead in the same manner - finger tips only. It's permissible to touch others during this one.
- Use different size balls. Start out with a larger beach ball - this seems easy. Progress through different sizes. Could you get your entire group around a golf ball?
- ADULTS ONLY - Every player gets a stick-pin. Travel with a balloon!!

ADDITIONAL **I**DEAS:

—THREE TARP ACTIVITIES

Note: For all the activities below, I use a 6' x 10' tarp. This progression works very well as a lead into the **Carpet Maze** initiative.

TARP ACTIVITY ONE: UNDER WHERE?

NEEDS: One 6' x 10' tarp (**Carpet Maze** tarp).

PROCEDURE: Set the opened tarp on the ground and ask everyone to get under the tarp without using any part of their arms from the elbow to fingertips. (I also prohibit the use of their mouth for lifting - because no one knows where the tarp has been.)

Assumptions may prevail during this one. When groups really go for the full "under" it's fun to watch. What is "under" anyway? Would everyone's toes be under?

OBSERVATIONS/QUESTIONS:
- Were you successful?
- Did anyone have an idea that was not heard or shared?
- What assumptions were made during the activity?
- What effects may "problem-solving" have on activities?
- Does anyone want to try another way of "under?"
(other) •
  •

ADDITIONAL IDEAS:

TARP ACTIVITY TWO: FLIPPER

NEEDS: One 6' x 10' tarp (**Carpet Maze** tarp). (A friend of mine uses a smaller size parachute and calls it "Paradigm Chute.")

PROCEDURE: Ask all the group members to stand on the tarp. (If you have more than 15 players, you'll need to use a bigger tarp.) The challenge will be to flip the tarp over and stand on the other side - without touching the ground in the process. Every player must be in contact with the tarp at all times.

OBSERVATIONS/QUESTIONS:
- What was the initial reaction of the group members?
- Who took a leadership role?
- What are "roles," and why are they important?
- What were some of the roles the group members took?
- Rate your success.

(other) •

•

ADDITIONAL IDEAS:

TARP ACTIVITY THREE: HALF-ZEES

NEEDS: One 6' x 10' tarp (**Carpet Maze** tarp), or a blanket works quite well too.

PROCEDURE: Progress to this one from **Flipper**. With the group standing on the tarp, ask them to fold the tarp in half without getting off. Tell them that quality will count. Discuss the qualities of quality when they have completed the first fold - is the tarp really in half? If they are up for another challenge, ask them to fold the tarp in half again - and yes, quality counts. How many times will the group be able to fold the tarp in half? Will the group know when they have reached their limit? As the tarp gets smaller, the group will be performing an activity similar to **Box Top** (see Elements).

OBSERVATIONS/QUESTIONS:
- What have been some common issues with all the activities?
- Is quality important?
- Were all the group members' needs met? Were they heard? Did people speak up for their needs? Is it important to speak up? Why?
- What have you learned that will help you work together more effectively in the future?
- What are some things you learned about each other?

(other) •

•

ADDITIONAL IDEAS:

STICKY SITUATION

Thanks to Sam Sikes.

NEEDS: One new roll of 1" masking tape. You will also want something to mark off a boundary area: rope, chairs, another roll of masking tape.

PROCEDURE: (Sam told me this one over the phone.) The boundaries for this one will depend upon the size of your group. So, read on to understand the process. Then determine the level of challenge you will present.

Have the group step into the boundary area. Discuss the importance of boundaries and why they are necessary. "Many times we have to do things with limited space. Let's see how well you will be able to adjust to limited space."

Hand someone the new roll of masking tape and give them this challenge: "Staying within the boundaries, completely unroll this roll of tape without breaking it. The only thing that can touch the tape in the process is skin. The only time the tape is allowed to touch itself is when it's coming off the roll."

As you might be able to imagine, the size of the working space will matter. The larger the space, the easier the initiative. But, who are we to make it easy for them? You could start big and then cut back. When does that ever happen?

OBSERVATIONS/QUESTIONS:
- What was the initial reaction of the group?
- What information was available to start with? What wasn't available?
- What planning took place?
- How were ideas shared within the group?
- What unforeseen problems came up? How were they dealt with?
- Did anyone make any sacrifices for the group? Did anyone refuse to make sacrifices? Why?
- What was the group's end result?
- Was the process worth the effort? What worth came out of the activity?
- Now what do you do with all this tape after it is unrolled?

(other) •

    •

VARIATIONS:
·How about rolling the tape back on to the roll? Too much?
·Can the group move out of the boundary area and pull the tape into a straight line?

ADDITIONAL **I**DEAS:
·Use the tape to make **Trash Balls** (see Appendix: Equipment Tricks, pg. 176)

—GOING NUTS—

NEEDS: One 5' section of 5/8" threaded rod and one 5/8" nut for each player (and if you want to add greater challenge, throw a few more in there). Set up the activity before hand by turning all the nuts onto the rod and leave them each at different places along the rod.

PROCEDURE: Present the rod to the group. Ask them to take the nuts off as fast as possible. One player to a nut or one nut to a player, either way is fine. That's it. Seems easy?

OBSERVATION/QUESTIONS:

- What was the group's initial reaction/expectation?
- What was the first problem encountered? What was the solution?
- Was there any sort of support during the activity? How did it help or hinder progress?
- When the first few players finished, what did they do? Does this same thing happen elsewhere?
- What was done with the rod after the nuts were removed? What can this be related to?
- Did anyone "Go Nuts?"

(other) •

•

VARIATIONS:

- My favorite. Have two rods in your equipment arsenal. Create, what I call, a One-Way Rod (say that three times fast), by carefully crimping the last few threads on one end (so it's hard to notice unless you really look). This will prevent the exit of nuts, thus the One-Way off concept. Most groups don't realize this until too late. WOW, what a processing plethora. Be ready for revolt!
- Number the nuts with a permanent marker. Turn them on in a random order. Once the group has them off, they must put them back on in order - 1, 2, 3, 4...... This is for time of course.
- I just thought of another ONE. Pit two small groups against each other, using the One-Way and Two-Way rods. What do you think will happen? I'm going to try this one as soon as possible.
- **Wing It** (Cain & Jolliff, 1998). This is a great small group variation (or a bunch of small groups at the same time). You can get 12" sections of 1/4" threaded rod already cut and ready to go from one of the larger hardware

stores. You'll need one of these and five wing nuts for every five people in your group. Use the ideas above on the small groups.

ADDITIONAL IDEAS:

RACCOON CIRCLES

Thanks to Tom Smith.

Tom Smith has been a very active Experiential Educator for many years. He has contributed several books to the field which have helped many facilitators to work more effectively with others. Tom developed a series of activities, which involve "circles." Tom writes, "The circle is often suggested as a symbol of unity, community, and connectedness, and it forms the basis for many activities of the challenge education program." These circle activities have grown to be a very effective and very popular way to explore the power and interaction of a group.

The "Circle" prop used for these activities is constructed from 1 inch tubular webbing. (A section of climbing rope will also work for most of the activities.) A standard size length is anywhere from 10 to 16 feet. Ten feet adds more challenge to the activities, a 16er will make it a little easier for the group. I tend to provide a circle for every 6 to 8 participants. With webbing in hand, tie the ends together with a water knot (a bowline for rope) to produce one continuous circle - this is the "Raccoon Circle" (singular).

After several different powerful experiences with these activities (my first with Tom), I started following this progression, adding some ideas of my own, with groups of 15 to 40 people. Please don't forget - **Safety** is always the first and most important goal.

Note: This progression starts with large group interaction, breaks into smaller groups, then ends with a couple of large group activities including a closure.

WHERE AM I?: Place an open Raccoon Circle (RC) on the ground (one for every 24 people). Ask each person to place one foot on the circle. Now without talking, rearrange the group so everyone is in alphabetical order. Oh yeah, without talking and, with one foot of each participant in contact with the webbing at all times. (I like to throw this one in the progression at different stages if I want to keep the "group" concept going. I'll use birthday order, middle name, or whatever.)

KNOT RACE: (Now break the group into small groups of 6 to 8 and give each group their own Raccoon Circle.) Use the knot in the webbing as a rabbit. Time how fast the group can get the knot around the circle and back to its starting position with every player touching the webbing. (It's interesting to see how groups define, "around and back.") Moving the knot to the right could be team "A." To the left could be team "B." Which team will put in a faster time?

Jim Cain offers this great variation. Using the knot as a pointer, begin the activity by revving up your motors, like a race car. Then squeel your tires (vocally) as the knot behaves like a race car going around the track - rapidly passing the webbing to the right. Slam on the breaks with a screech. Ask the person closest to the knot to answer a get-aquainted question, such as, "What is your favorite color?" Then squeal the tires again, and you're off in the opposite direction. Screeeeeech, "What is your......?"

OVER AND **O**UT: Set the RC down in a wide open position. The players are asked to stand inside the circle, facing in, holding hands. The objective will be to pick up the RC, bring it over everybody's head and drop it into the center of the group - without using any hands. For a bit more challenge, I ask that the arms be still if the webbing is touching them. You can do "Over and In," too.

LEANERS: (Moving into some trust and safety issues now.) Circle the group facing in with both hands on the webbing - without pulling (this can be a challenge in itself). Ask the players to lean back as far as possible and find a place where everyone is in balance with feet together. How far can the group members, a little at a time, walk their feet in toward the middle of the circle. Discuss problem-solving and how it can benefit the group. What is balance? What is important about balance?

CIRCLE **S**IT & **S**TAND: From **Leaners**, have the group sit down without letting go of the webbing and without moving their feet (which are together). Make sure you emphasize going slowly to prevent them from dropping too hard on their butts. Stand up with the same restrictions. It's also fun to add some sounds for going down and up - sharing with the other groups is good too. Put a few ups and downs together. Ask the group how they think they will get through the ups and downs of their program.

Moving on, I ask the group to tie an over-hand knot into the middle of the Raccoon Circle to form what is now, "<u>Raccoon Circles</u>." (The closer the two circles are to the same size the better - but hey, to each their own!) I also like to make sure the initial knot is at one end of the loops before the overhand goes in (see diagram).

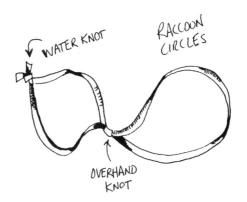

WATER KNOT

RACCOON CIRCLES

OVERHAND KNOT

CIRCLE THE **C**IRCLE: (Rohnke, "Silver Bullets") Circle the group, holding hands, facing in. Double up the RC so there is just one double circle. Start with the doubled RC between two of the players (these players should be holding hands through the RC). Now have the group move through the RC one person at a time until the RC has traveled around the entire group and back to the starting spot without using or breaking loose of hands. Try this one with players facing out (thanks Don B.)

DUAL **D**IRECTIONS: Start the double circle between two players again. This time one circle goes to the left, the other to the right. This is where the original water knot comes in handy. If the water knot was at one end when you tied the overhand knot in the racoon circle, then the water knot can be used to identify a direction. When the circles cross at the opposite end of the group it will be easy to keep track of the knot continuing in the same direction. How about this - blindfold all but two players - one sighted player directs one circle, the other, the other circle- or can the sighted person direct both circles/projects?

GEAR **B**OX: (Bringing the groups together.) With the **Circle the Circle** concept in mind, bring the small groups closer together. Have each group hold hands facing in. Now attach the RCs between small groups - one loop from the dual circle attached between two players of one group, the other circle between two players from another group. Go around the area connecting groups in this manner until ALL groups are connected with only two circles. Make sure there are at least two to three players between each connection (see diagram). Now, with the gear turning (for the most part) concept, have group members move through the circles with this idea - a player from each group must move through each circle at the same time until everyone has passed through both circles of their group. A VERY challenging group communication task.

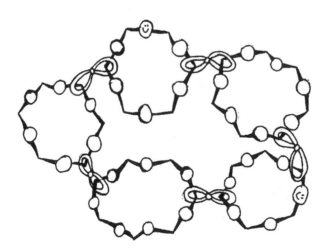

22

THE COMMUNITY CIRCLE: (Tom Smith) Untie the overhand knot from the webbing and have small groups do the **Circle Sit & Stand** again on their own. (The tone for this conclusion should be somewhat serious.) Still keep safety a high priority. When all the groups are ready, "...there can be a closing ceremony that involves overlapping the smaller circles into one large circle. This involves one person from each circle ducking under the web loop of another group, so there will be connected circles (see diagram). If there are five or six groups a big circle made up of smaller circles can be formed. Can all the groups do a balanced and cooperative Sit & Stand together? Three in a row? With sound effects? In a wave?"

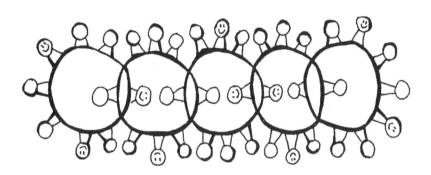

As with any Experiential activity, wrap up with some processing of the experience. I will leave the Observations/Questions up to you on this one. What was the power of the circle? Tom has a small book available that includes the philosophy of "circles," more activities and some wonderful closing ideas, including the "Tale of the Sands" (see References section for details).

VARIATIONS:

ADDITIONAL **I**DEAS:
   • Webbing can also be used with: **Birthday Rope, Rope Bus, Mine Field, Trash Collectors, Swamp Walk, The Cube** & **Roof Tops**.

NEEDS: One small object, like a coin or a rock, and a small area to play.

PROCEDURE: Stand in a small, shoulder-to-shoulder circle facing in. Choose a player to be in the center. Have the circled players bend their elbows, extending their forearms into the circle with their hands palm down, in a fist. The center player covers his/her eyes while the leader gives the small object to one of the circled players. When the object is within the circle, the center player can uncover his/her eyes. The objective of the circled players is to pass the object (IT) around the circle, each person touching IT, until IT is back to the original starting point, without the center player finding IT. Passes happen when a player with the object taps the top of another player's hand. This player turns up his/her open hand, the passer drops the object into the open hand. The receiver closes and turns his/her hand back down. Fake passes can happen to throw the center player off the track. Noises are also permitted to distract the guesser. Center player has 3 guesses. Circle players have 1 minutes to get It around. GO!

OBSERVATIONS/QUESTIONS:
    • Did you feel uncomfortable in the center?
    • What do you think made it uncomfortable?
    • Why was it hard to pick someone?
    • What other situations make you uncomfortable?
    • How did it feel to find the object?
    • How did it feel not to find the object? What made it hard to find?
    • Are you easily distracted? What do you do when you get distracted?
(other) •
        •

VARIATION:
    • Play with a small ball that has a bell inside - this is tough!
    • I like this one. Use a long length (large enough for your group to get around) of thin rope - I use a 1/4" size. Put the rope through a ring or washer and tie the ends. (Make sure the ring can fit over the knot that's tied in the rope.) Now have the players grasp the rope with both hands with the hand of one player covering the ring. Pass the ring by sliding it around the rope.

ADDITIONAL IDEAS:

NAME BALL

Thanks to Frank Harris and Fearon Teacher Aids.

NEEDS: Two different colored lightweight balls and a mid-size open area. I like to use some spots for players to stand on - but they are not needed.

PROCEDURE: Players stand in a circle, facing in, with space to permit catching and throwing a ball in any direction. This will be position "A". Each player learns the first name of the players on their left and right. Hand one of the players a ball. This lead player then names the person on his right and tosses the ball (henceforth designated as the "right ball") to that player. The ball is passed consecutively to the right, as each thrower names the person to whom he throws. The ball may be passed around the circle two or three times, so that players become familiar with each other's names. The facilitator then removes the "right ball" from the circle.

Using a different colored ball, a lead player tosses it to the player on his left, (henceforth the "left ball") saying this player's name. This ball is also passed consecutively to the left, as each thrower names the person to whom he is throwing. Again, the group can do this a few times around to get the names down. The facilitator then removes the "left ball" from the circle and hands the "right ball" back to any player.

Before the throwing starts again, ask the players to scramble around to different positions in the circle (not standing next to the same players they just left - or right!?). This is position "B". The player with the "right ball" locates the person who was on his right in position "A," names that person, and tosses the ball to that person. That player in turn does the same thing with the player who was on his right in position "A." Continue this tossing process. Should a player miss a catch for any reason, that player or another player may pick the ball up and resume play, tossing to the "right" person.

When the passing is well along, add the "left ball." The first player with the ball finds the player that was on his left before the scrambling took place. Keep both balls going in their specified directions. Don't forget about name calling - not the bad kind either!

Once the game is well under way, additional "left" and "right" balls may be used. I try to stick with the same color for each direction, but that's me. Players can also be asked to change places more than once.

OBSERVATIONS/**Q**UESTIONS:
- What was hard about the activity?
- What would have made the activity run smoother?
- Did anyone become confused during the game? How did you react?
- Is it okay to get confused? What makes it not okay?
- What might be the lesson learned here?

(other) •

      •

VARIATIONS:
- Add a rubber chicken to the circle. No one wants the rubber chicken so they are going to throw it to someone else - to anyone. What does the rubber chicken do to the process? What might you guess the rubber chicken represents? What sorts of "rubber chickens" turn up in your life?
- How fast can the group return to position "A"? This is how I say it: "I'm going to time this next challenge. How fast can you return to position "A"? - GO!

ADDITIONAL **I**DEAS:
- **Name Ball** props can also be used with: **Mine Field, Trash Collector,** & other ball-tossing activities.

MOON BALL

Thanks to Karl Rohnke, "The Bottomless Bag Again."

NEEDS: One medium-size beach ball and a large open area.

PROCEDURE: Scatter the group around the open area. Using a fully inflated beach ball, the group's objective is to strike the ball aloft as many times as possible before the ball touches the ground. Players are not allowed to strike the ball twice in succession. A hand strike counts as 1 loft point, a head strike counts as 2 loft points. Set a loft point goal to reach. Play a few times trying to break previously set marks.

I often do a bit of problem-solving before each new game. This gives the group a chance to make a plan. I try to end the activity after a successful, goal-breaking game.

OBSERVATIONS/QUESTIONS:
- How many thought the activity would be easy?
- What sorts of problems did you encounter? How did you solve them?
- Was there any leadership?
- How did you feel as you got closer to your goal?
- How did it feel to fall short of your goal? Did anyone get discouraged?
- What was it like to surpass your goal?

(other) •

•

VARIATIONS:
- Hit the ball in sequence without letting it hit the ground. No one hits it again until every player has hit it once. How many hits can you get?
- How fast can a ball travel from player to player in sequence?
- How many times can the ball be hit in one minute?
- Spread some hula-hoops around the playing area. Players must have a foot in a hoop when striking the ball.

ADDITIONAL IDEAS:
- Beach Balls can also be used with: **Zig-Zag, Up in the Air, Islands, Mine Field,** & **Trash Collector.**

ZIG-ZAG

NEEDS: Two mid-size throwable objects and a small open space.

PROCEDURE: Split the group in half and form 2 lines, facing each other about 10' apart. Any extra person can choose either line. Start 1 throwable object at different ends of each line (1 object per line). Time how long it takes to pass the objects diagonally across from 1 person to the next, down the lines, and back to the objects' original starting point. Each group member must catch each object twice. Each player must receive the ball from a player in the other line.

This is a pretty straight forward initiative; however, watch out for rule manipulation from experienced groups. I often use this game with newer groups who have not figured out guideline variations (or what some others call creative manipulation). Some groups spend more time trying to figuring out what the catch is than actually doing the activity. There is no real catch to this one - that I have seen. (YET!)

OBSERVATIONS/QUESTIONS:
- What did it take to be successful?
- What are some components of teamwork?
- What was difficult about the activity?
- How did you solve the problems that came up?
- Was there any planning involved?
- Is planning important?
- Does a time pressure affect performance? Why do you think so?

(other) •

•

VARIATIONS:
- Use four objects. Start one at each end of both lines.
- Use different types of objects: a milk jug, waste basket, blanket, and a watermelon (a small one to make it fair).
- Use balloons to bat back and forth.
- We can't forget water balloons or eggs!

ADDITIONAL IDEAS:
- **Zig-Zag** equipment can also be used with: **Mine Field, Trash Collectors** & other ball-tossing activities.

NEEDS: One ricochet ball for a group of up to 10 players - more players, more balls. I've done my best to draw a picture of the ball. The closest thing you can find to a "real" ricochet ball would be in one of the larger pet store chains. I've seen them called "space balls" or "star balls." To get a real "human" one call KYTEC at 800-732-4883, ask for their Reaction Ball. (Some of the Sports Equipment Catalogs carry the Z-Ball. Project Adventure has them too. You can find the numbers for these catalogs in the Appendix section.) Contact Chris for his new book on "Games With an Odd Ball."

This is sort of what it looks like!?

INTRODUCTION: The original game was developed for competitive play (directions in the Variations section). From the suggestion of a friend, Craig Dobkin, I created some cooperative versions that have turned out to be just as fun.

PROCEDURE: First you need some of the lingo if you want to go international.

Point - Each time the ball strikes the surface of the **Span**.

Rocket - A throw as high as the thrower can throw-it-up. Accuracy will also count, and overhead space will be a factor.

Sneaker - The lowest throw allowed: about as high as the tallest player. (This term comes from the gamester, Karl Rohnke. A little more fun than the original so I kept it - thanks Karl!)

Skyscraper - A throw in between a Rocket and a Sneaker.

Ricochet - When the ball angles drastically away from the potential catcher after the first bounce.

Back-Lash - When the ball angles drastically back toward the catcher after the first bounce. (Karl Rohnke has dubbed this the "Cup Carom" and suggests to both males and females that they adorn themselves for safety in the relevant places.)

Rabbit - When the ball takes off on a low trajectory at a fast pace exhibiting a number of fast, hard to catch-up-to bounces.

Roller - Considered a 'dead' ball. The ball dribbles close to the ground when bounces are no longer countable.

Dud - A ball that comes to a dead stop after hitting a soft surface.

Span - This is the playing surface for the game. It could be a section of sidewalk, street, basketball court or for faster action, a racquetball court (or anything else similar). My friend Brian boasts the first game on ICE.

For **Cooperative Ricochet**, you'll set up your group just like Ricochet on the following page, but this time you'll be going for a group score (I've done this version with up to 10 players). After setting up the order of throwers and catchers, ask each player how many points he or she is going to catch for the team in the round. Add up every player's points for the group goal. Then play the game. Players may reach their goal, fall short or exceed their mark. (All wonderful areas to explore in the processing to follow.)

I have found the most effective time to use this activity is right after a break. I'll start with a few players and as soon as we get going, the nature and action of the game draws other players in. All we do is ask them how many points they plan to catch, add that to what we have and then "play on."

OBSERVATIONS/QUESTIONS:
- What were your expectations before the game? Were they met?
- Were you able to reach your goal?
- What is important to consider when goal setting?
- If we played the game again, what sort of goal would you set?
- What is the role of "chance" in this activity? How do you play into the roll of chance?
- Being one of the last catchers, were there any outside expectations imposed on you? Were there any extra internal expectations you imposed on yourself?
- What made the game fun?

(other) •
  •

ANOTHER COOPERATIVE VARIATION:

Break Out - For this one you need a large circle on your span. I use an activity rope if there isn't a painted circle (found on a basketball court). Players position themselves around the outside of the circle and cannot step into the circle at any time during the game. One player starts with a Sneaker into the circle - all throws are Sneakers during this game. The objective is to count Points that touch in the circle. Keep this game fast paced with throws shortly after catches. Add Points as you continue play. When the ball "breaks out" of the circle and touches the ground outside the circle, the game ends. The Points you have acquired will be the record to break for the next game. This game's "degree of difficulty" is related to the number of players around the circle or the "size-of-circle-to-player-quotient."

My friend Sam plays **Break Out** inside, using a table top. You can also use your **Mountain Tops** platforms (see Elements section) if you're out on the course.

COMPETITIVE VARIATION:

Ricochet - A good number of players for this game is 2 to 6 per ball. Circle up all the players on the Span and number off in circular order. (Give yourselves a lot of room.) This will be the throwing order for the remainder of the game. Choose a game closing score: 10 points is an average short game. First player to 10 wins the game (of course winning by two). To begin, player #1 takes the ball. Player #2 calls one of the 3 throws. The thrower honors the call with as accurate a toss as possible, and aims toward striking the ground close to the center of the group. The catcher (# 2) can call a re-throw before the ball strikes the span if it looks like an errant throw. Each time the ball strikes the span, a Point is counted: that is IF the catcher catches the ball before it becomes a Roller or a Dud. (The trick is knowing when to catch it.) The total number of bounces makes up the score for that throw after a successful catch. During this bounding pursuit, the other players do their best to stay out of the way. (They can help count bounces and determine Rollers.) If a ball hits ANY player by mistake, it is considered a Dud, and that play is over with no score recorded. However, subtract 1 point from the player it hit. Player #2 then throws for player #3 and so on. To end the game, a player must be ahead of everyone by 2 points. You can have over 10 points scored, but everyone has 1 more try to catch the leader. If a new leader emerges - another round - and so on, until someone has won by 2. OR just play to 10.

If you can obtain or already have a copy of "Quicksilver" by Karl Rohnke and Steve Butler, turn to page 133 for some added fun to Ricochet.

ADDITIONAL IDEAS:

─BOUNDARY BALL─

This is a long one, but well worth the time and energy!

NEEDS: For a group of 12 you will need: 12 hula-hoops (or rope circles), 30 spot markers (cardboard, coffee can lids, Spots), 96 small throwable objects; 8 of a kind (e.g., wadded paper, sponges, foam balls, stuffed animals, ping-pong balls, tennis balls), 1 large basket or container that will hold the 96 objects, and a medium-size open area.

PROCEDURE: Set up the gear according to the diagram below. Each hula-hoop should contain a spot to stand on and 8 identical objects. (I like to vary the objects from circle to circle. The reason will come up in a minute.) Set the extra spots around the playing area and place the container somewhere in the middle of everything (for now).

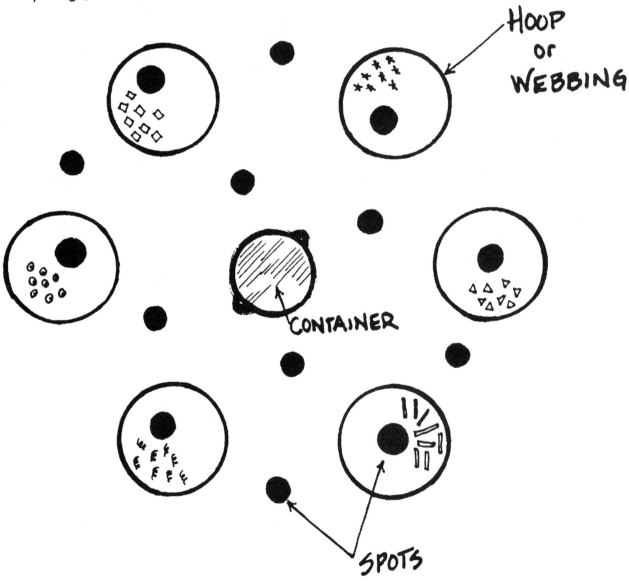

HOOP
or
WEBBING

CONTAINER

SPOTS

The main activity objective is following directions. (You can also work with goal setting.) Before sending the participants into the playing area, tell them to choose a circle with small objects in it and stand on the spot within that circle - this will be boundary #1. Send them to the playing area and watch what happens. Do they do anything else? Are they "following directions?" Ask everyone to count their objects, without touching them, to make sure there are 8. Tell the group they will be tossing their objects in an attempt to make them stay within the large container. Before you start, ask each player to tell you how many objects they will get into the container (goal setting). Restate these 2 directions before starting each round: 1) Each person must stand within their boundary with both feet until the leader states the round is OVER, and 2) the players are only allowed to throw the objects that are within their hula-hoop. "So what if other objects enter my hoop?" I will restate the directions for them. (What do you think?)

When questions come up, 90% of the time I repeat the "Directions." (This drives them crazy.) I want to see how players interpret the directions. If there are concerns of safety, I will address them.

The only time I would stop before the objects are no longer flying is when there is a safety problem. Usually it involves throwing harder objects "too hard," and hitting other players across the activity area. Otherwise, I continue until everyone is standing still on their spots and there are no more objects flying about. I call the round OVER. From here we discuss how they did with their goals and some reasons for success or failure. Then I ask everyone to gather the objects they started with, put them in their circle, and stand within their boundary.

Before the next round begins, I do a couple of things. First, I ask if anyone would like to trade circles with another player before the next round (no one likes the sponges). Both players must agree. (Think about what you could process about trading. Why? Being friendly? More challenging? Less challenging?) Then we talk about who followed the 2 stated directions during the previous round. This is always fun. (As the round is being played, try and pick up as many violations as possible because some players do not realize they are not following directions.) If they violated a rule they must stay within the same boundary of the previous round (i.e., for round two they would need to remain with boundary #1, the spot within the circle). If they followed both directions last round, their new boundary becomes the entire hoop or small rope circle - this is boundary #2. Restate the 2 directions, ask for each player's goals and begin again.

Continue the process. When a player follows directions, expand the boundaries (e.g., reach for objects outside their hula hoop without touching the ground, reach out for other objects allowing them to touch the ground, step out of the circle onto any spot, toss any object, travel to any spot.)

You can stop the activity after any round. I like to ask if the players want to play again. This way I can pick up the energy level. **Boundary Ball** is a great game to EXPERIENCE the benefit of following directions. It has also given me a great reference point to go back to during a program when directions are really important - aren't they always!

OBSERVATIONS/QUESTIONS:
- Were players able to follow the first direction and not touch objects?
- What was the hardest direction to follow? Why?
- Did anyone add to directions? Why?
- Did players reach outside their circle for objects?
- Did players throw objects that landed in their circle? Was that okay?
- Did players reach their goals? What were the factors involved?
- Why did players want to switch? Who did they ask?
- Why were they willing to switch? Not willing?
- What reactions/feelings occurred with objects difficult to throw?
- Did players adjust their goals according to the type of objects?
- What happened when you didn't follow directions?
- What happened when you did follow directions?
- Why is following directions important?

(other) ·

·

VARIATIONS:
- Ask players with difficult objects to throw, if there is anything they could ask to make the activity easier for them. You, as the leader, can choose to grant their request or not. (What I'm looking for is "move the basket closer" - maybe I do, maybe I don't.) Work on asking.
- Blindfolding players is another interesting variation. How does this affect their goal setting?
- Start out the game with some players having more objects than others. How does this relate to social situations - discrimination? Affluence?
- Start out the game with some players having larger boundaries. What does this bring up?

ADDITIONAL IDEAS:
- **Boundary Ball** equipment can also be used with: **Lily Pads, Chris-Cross, Mine Field, Trash Collector, Electiric Porthole, Roof Tops** & other ball-tossing activities.

FIREBALL

Thanks to Brian Brolin.

This is an adaptation of a traditional "Honor" game played by some American Indian tribes. They often played games like **Fireball** and **Flinch** (see p. 39) to teach the concepts of honor and respect.

NEEDS: One small throwable object (an authentic fire ball was made from deerskin with seeds or small stones inside), and a medium size area.

PROCEDURE: Players form a large circle (two arms length) and toss the ball to each other following these rules:

1) Players cannot make any vocal noises.
2) Players cannot make a bad catch.
3) Players cannot make a bad throw.

After a few games add this rule:

4) If the leader points at a player, that player must kneel down.

Do not define the rules for the players. If they ask, just say, "It is up to you and only you." Observe how rules are interpreted. If a rule is broken, the player must step back from the circle and kneel down on one knee. These players are no longer allowed to catch or throw the fireball. The game continues until only 2 or 3 players remain. Stress the point that it is the individual's choice to kneel down, being a test of honesty and honor within themselves.

Brian likes to present the game this way: "This is a game of honor. Honor is not easy to achieve. It is held in the minds of others about you, from watching what you do. In this game a fact is a fact; a bad throw is a bad throw; a bad catch is a bad catch; a noise is a noise. Others will see this and judge you for your choices. Their interpretation may be more important than yours. In the end, however, you must decide!" (Something of this nature.)

OBSERVATIONS/QUESTIONS:
- Why did you kneel down?
- If you knelt down, did you lose? If you follow the rules do you lose?
- Should someone have knelt down who didn't? What did you do?
- To whom does the choice belong?
- What were individual definitions of the rules?
- What is at stake if people stretch or break the rules?

· What sort of reputation might that person obtain?
· Is it easy to change a reputation? What would it take?
· What is "Honor"?
· How do you obtain honor?
· Why is honor important?
· Is there anyone you know who possesses honor?
· How did you feel/react when the leader pointed at you to kneel?
· Why do you think the leader pointed at you?

(other) ·

 ·

(See **Flinch** for more questions.)

ADDITIONAL IDEAS:

FLINCH

Thanks to Brian Brolin.

NEEDS: One small throwable object (a fire ball if you have one), and a medium-size area to play.

PROCEDURE: Form a large circle with the leader in the center. Players stand perfectly still with arms crossed in front of them facing the leader. Give these rules:

1) Players cannot move except to catch and throw the object.
2) Players cannot make any sounds during the game.

The leader tosses the object randomly at players. Be sure to turn around enough to interact with everyone. Players must catch the object, throw it back to the leader, and then recross their arms. The leader can fake a toss to a player also. If the player moves or makes a sound when there has been no throw, he or she must back out of the circle and kneel down on one knee. The game continues until only 2 or 3 players are left standing.

Just as in **Fireball**, players are ultimately responsible for themselves. **Flinch** is a game that can build honor and trust.

OBSERVATIONS/QUESTIONS:
- Was it hard to play this game? What made it hard?
- What reason did you have for kneeling?
- Did anyone influence your decision to kneel?
- What was some of the self-talk in your head during the game? Where do you think self-talk comes from?
- What is important about following directions?
- What kind of person follows directions? What kind of person doesn't?
- What kind of person do you want to be seen as? Why?
- Are other people's opinions important to you? Why?

(other) •
        •

(See **Fireball** for more questions.)

VARIATIONS:
- I like to play non-elimination **Flinch**. If a player breaks a rule the first time, place hands on hips; the second time, hands on head; the third time,

37

hands on knees. If any player reaches the third phase, I usually start a new game with one of the players becoming the leader. Then I take a spot in the circle.

•With a small group, have the players line up in front of the leader in a semi-circle shape.

ADDITIONAL **I**DEAS:

NEEDS: This activity does require a variety of objects that can be volleyed up into the air. I use one 47" beach ball, a few medium-size beach balls and a couple of small ones. I also include a "Wacky" ball, the kind you blow up and it doesn't fly straight, a couple of blow-up rings and a few balloons. (Whatever you use, be sure to use objects that would not hurt if they bopped you in the head. Be creative.)

PROCEDURE: I really wanted to add this game because it has been such a metaphorical winner for me. I hope you will be able to find the resources so you can try this yourself.

Each object used represents a hypothetical problem which the group must handle. They soon find out that some problems slip through the cracks. How will the group handle such "problems?"

I like to start with the largest beach ball (which, by the way, takes a great deal of time to blow up the old fashioned way). I have the group scattered around a large open area. I toss the big ball out into the group and ask them to keep hitting it up into the air as long as they can (as in **Moon Ball**, p. 29 - a good lead-in activity).

After a short time, I add another object, then another, and another, until all the objects are in the center (somewhere). I continue to demand that all the objects need to be up off the ground. I let the group play for a while to see what happens to the different objects. Then I ask them to stop and let the objects fall to the ground. I circle the group around the objects and dive into the process.

One of my most memorable processing experiences happened when the sun created a large shadow off of the largest beach ball. "Sometimes the more obvious problems overshadow the less obvious. What skills will we need to recognize the less obvious problems as we move along?" And so it goes!!

OBSERVATIONS/**Q**UESTIONS:
  • When was the game easy? Why?
  • When was it hard? What made it harder?
  • Let's pretend each object was a problem you had to solve by keeping it in the air. Which problems were easy?
  • What happened to the little problems?
  • What can happen if we neglect little problems?
  • How were group members taking care of the little problems?
  • What ideas could you come up with to take care of little problems?
  • Did anyone have to remind you about the little problems?
  • Do you like being reminded about things?

•In what way would you like people to remind you?

(other) •

        •

VARIATIONS:
   •Blindfold someone in the group. This is a powerful processing piece. I stand next to the person as a body protector, but I don't instruct at all. Will anyone help the one who is in need? If you blindfold someone after the game gets started, will anyone notice?
   •See "Balloon Frantic," Rohnke, 1994.
   •See "Balloon Foosball," Sikes, 1998, if you have a really big group and want one of those "bat-things-up-in-the-air" games.

ADDITIONAL **I**DEAS:
   •**Up in the Air** equipment can also be used with: **Moon Ball, Zig-Zag, Mine Field,** and other ball-tossing activities.

NEEDS: Two pairs of balled-up socks as throwing implements, 4 boundary markers, and an open area.

PROCEDURE: This is one of my favorite experientials (when it works). The trick is to get players to realize they need help to succeed in this game. However, realization doesn't always happen. There are times when I will probe into problem-solving a little early so they "get it."

This game is ideal for groups of 8 to 12 players. Set up 15' x 25' boundary lines and have the group stand inside. Present them with this lead-in story:

> "I need one brave volunteer to be the King of the Outtees (Queen works too). Thank you very much! The King here has the task of turning all of you Innees (inside the rectangle community) into Outtees. The King cannot enter into the Innee kingdom, so he must throw this magic sock to transform his subjects. However, the only vulnerable place of an Innee is their BUTT, thus by being *SOCKED IN THE BUTT*, the Innee becomes an Outtee and steps out of the Innee kingdom to Outtee land. The new Outtee helps the King to transform more Innees to Outtees. Of course by the rules of fair play, Innees are not allowed to Butt Block (BB) in any way: sitting, standing back to back, forming a circle or hand-blocking. If caught, "BahBing," the player automatically becomes an Outtee. Also, if an Innee steps out of the kingdom, he or she is transformed into an Outtee. One last point, no one wants a dirty old sock in their kingdom - if the magic sock lands in the kingdom of Inn, it is good gamespersonship to carefully kick or toss the sock back to one of the Outtees. Who knows, maybe they will have mercy on you and leave you to be the last Innee, making you King of the Innee kingdom!"

In layman's terms, the player(s) on the outside must hit the players on the inside by throwing a sock-ball at their gluteus maximal areas.

When the concept works, you may hear something I have heard from participants, "I can't do this by myself." I respond with, "So, what can you do?" The problem-solving begins. I have had the King of the Outtees ask if any of the Innees wanted to be an Outtee - asking for help! (How many of us need work on this issue?)

Outtees are allowed to toss the sock ball to each other for stategic purposes. (In fact, we hope that happens - teamwork and all that stuff.) When there are a few Outtees in the ranks, I add the other sock. Things really start moving then. Play until 1 Innee remains.

OBSERVATIONS/**Q**UESTIONS:

·How successful was the lone King of the Outtees?
·Did the King ask for help? Who helped?
·Did any of the Innees take any chances? Why?
·What did it take to become more successful?
·Who won the activity? Was it important to win?
·What is important about teamwork? What does teamwork involve?
·Was there any planning among the Outtees?
·Did the Innees make any plans?

(other) ·
        ·

VARIATIONS:

·Sock in the foot, the back, the leg. (Please, no sock in the mouth!)

ADDITIONAL **I**DEAS:

·**Sock in the Butt** equipment can also be used with: **Mine Field** & **Trash Collector.**

NEEDS: Two soft throwable objects, no larger than a softball, for each person and an area for a large circle (or whatever the group forms). Tennis balls from **Tennis Ball Walk** work well.

PROCEDURE: Start the group in a large circle. Each player's objective will be to throw 2 objects to another player in the group <u>at the same time</u>. (See the variations for an easier version to start with if needed.) Players can only receive a throw from someone they are not throwing to. Also, any 1 player may only possess 2 objects at one time. How many throws can your group achieve, in a row, without dropping an object?

Seems simple enough? After giving the directions, this is a great one to sit back and watch. I have seen large groups fragment into smaller groups. This is fine, but make sure the rules are being followed. If they are successful with small groups, ask them to try the activity again in a large group to see what happens.

I have found that walking around the group(s) as they are working keeps individuals on track. It also gives them opportunities to ask questions, and of course you will encourage them to ask the group.

OBSERVATIONS/**Q**UESTIONS:
- What roles did people take?
- Who took leadership roles?
- Were ideas being heard?
- Which individuals were initially reactive to the activity?
- What forms of reaction were there?
- How did the group communicate with each other?
- What made the activity challenging?
- Was there anything you could do to eliminate the problems your group encountered?
- What was the advantage of splitting into small groups (if it happened)?
- How successful were you in small or large groups?

(other) •
         •

VARIATIONS:
- Start out with one object each and progress from there (be sure to try some people with two objects and others with one - it's a blast).
- If you have enough bouncable objects, try a one bounce-and-catch progression.

ADDITIONAL **I**DEAS:
- **Objectables** equipment can also be used with: **Boundary Ball, Mine Field, Trash Collectors, Tennis Ball Walk,** & other ball-tossing activities.

LILY PADS & ISLANDS

NEEDS: Spot markers (anything safe to stand on - plastic canvases, place mats, foam shelf liner) and some Hula-Hoops. The number of each will be determined by your objective for the activity. To start, each player will either be standing on a spot (Lily Pad) or in a hula-hoop (Island). As the game progresses, you will take away Lily Pads until only Islands are left with everyone on the Islands. So decide how many Islands your group will be able to fit onto safely and use that number. If you overestimated, you can take away Islands after all the Lily Pads are gone. I set up the activity in a large area scattering spots and hoops about haphazardly, then ask each player to find their own Lily Pad or Island to stand on.

Note: Plastic Canvases are found in craft stores. Also, the newest thing I've found for slippery floor areas is the foam shelf liner.

PROCEDURE: I like to use this activity to start out programs. There's warm-up and initiative potential here. This game can produce a lot of frantic running where collisions are possible. So when I have every player's attention, we talk about safety (I usually spend a little more time with younger groups on this topic). If worse comes to worse and I have to slow them way down, I'll have them put bean bags on their heads and tell them they cannot move without the bean bag remaining on their head (of course they can't hold it on).

Have each player stand on a Lily Pad or an Island (there should be a spot or hoop for everyone). Before each round ask: Are both feet on a Lily Pad or within an Island? When the answer is "yes," the next round is called. The action of the game involves moving from Lily Pad to Lily Pad or Lily Pad to Island, Island to Lily Pad, or Island to Island, when you say the key word (this can be any word you choose). Although not a timed or competitive event, players seem to think it is.)

Once a few safe rounds have been played, with enough places for everyone, I have often (actually every time, come to think of it) had to re-do the safety talk. Sometimes we will even do the Safety Oath: Raise your right foot - repeat after me, "I, (state your name), promise to be safe and..." (you get the idea here).

After the guideline check, the game begins again, but this time I start to remove Lily Pads. This of course causes dissonance because their "mental model" is that each person has their own place. (Initially, I'll take away just one Lily Pad so that I can process with this first person left without a spot, then I'll take a couple at a time.) Problem-solving occurs (sometimes with a nudge), and they start to share. As you progress, the Islands get a bit more crowded.

Before it comes down to everyone on an Island, I will ask again, "Who remembers what is most important?" (I hope 'safety' popped into your head). Then we try everyone on the Islands (or Island).

The group has just participated in an initiative. So we can use this frame of reference to base future activities on. Hopefully there was some success, maybe some learning about safety, maybe some teamwork.

OBSERVATIONS/QUESTIONS:
- Was the activity fun? What made it fun or not fun?
- What was the most important part of the activity? Why?
- What learnings came from that activity - for you?
- How did you feel being the first player without a spot?
- How was the problem resolved? How did you feel then?
- What is important about sharing?
- Describe the reactions when Lily Pads were disappearing. How did the "change" affect you?
- What was it like being together on the Island(s)?
- Can this togetherness create more support during "change?" How?
- What can we do to continue or change what happened?

(other) •

•

VARIATIONS:
- Can everyone in the group be in one hula-hoop following the guideline? (This is possible if everyone sits on the floor and sticks both feet into the hoop.) What is "within the hoop?"
- Working with Corporate groups I have called this Cubicles and Corner Offices. When resources are taken away, I have used the metaphor of "downsizing" or "Resource Management."
- Blindfold a few players. Who will be helpful? (I have only done this with safe groups - players who have learned to trust each other over time.)
- You could also use **Racoon Circle** webbing instead of hula-hoops. It's much easier to travel with (unless you have the $$ for those sectioned hula-hoops).

ADDITIONAL IDEAS:
- **Lily Pads & Islands** equipment can also be used with: **Corporate Box, Chris-Cross, Boundary Ball, Descend-sion** (with Hoops), & **Mine Field**.

NEEDS: You will want to prepare at least 2 different puzzles with enough pieces for each person in the group to have at least 1 piece. I use the large panels of 2 <u>identical</u> cereal boxes (you will see why in a second). If you want, cut the pictures in crazy puzzle shapes. Be careful to keep the 2 pictures' pieces separate (for now). I have used a paper cutter to cut angled shapes and it works out just great.

PROCEDURE: Place 1 dismantled puzzle in a box or bag and bring it to the group. Conceal a few of the second puzzle pieces in your pocket for later. Present the boxed puzzle pieces to the group. Have each person remove 1 piece at a time until all are gone (some players may end up with more than one piece). Tell the group you will time them to see how long it takes to put the puzzle together; each group member adding his or her own puzzle pieces to the final picture.

Try another attempt after collecting and redistributing the pieces, to see if the group can better their time. Usually the group will want to try again. On a third attempt, I "secretly" trade the pieces in my pocket for some in the box (you've got to be sneaky - you don't want to get caught or the lesson may be lost). Then start them off. <u>Be ready</u> for anything here. I have experienced everything from anger to laughter depending on the population. Process the reactions.

OBSERVATIONS/QUESTIONS:
- Describe what the activity was like for you.
- What sorts of communication did you use?..or not use?
- What reactions took place on the trial with different pieces?
- Is this your common reaction to change?
- Can you completely stop change from happening?
- What can you do to "change" your reaction to change?
- Do you want to try the activity again with the proper pieces?..or 2 puzzles?
(other) •
         •

VARIATIONS:
- Clifford Knapp (1988) uses a large leaf, the single blade kind (not the compound kind). Tear the leaf up into pieces and follow the procedure above. Mr. Knapp also likes to do the activity without verbal communication.
- This activity would surely work with a small manufactured puzzle. Avoid the 1000 piecers, it may take too long.
- The newest variation I have tried is with 2" by 4" wooden blocks. Cut enough pieces of board to make a pretty good size square. Then cut each board into

3 parts (of different lengths). Sand the pieces up a bit to make it nice, then use the pieces for your puzzle. (See diagram.)

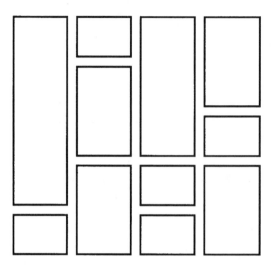

•I call this the **Big Foot Puzzle**. My friend Scott Trent has a great puzzle. It's a good deal of work, but the activity is great - one of the best closing activities I have ever seen. Scott cuts up a 4' x 4' piece of plywood into 16 puzzle pieces that interlock (this is the work part). Then he bores out 2 - 1" holes in each piece. Through the holes he adds a foot strap (webbing and a clip). Now the players have to attach a puzzle piece (or 2) to their feet, then solve the puzzle. Call Scott for more details - and find out about his great portable Organizational Building Blocks. Scott's number is found in the "Additional Experiential Resources" section.
•**NEAT Puzzle**. A great puzzle activity found in Karl Rohnke's "FUNN Stuff, Volume One" (see, Rohnke Resources in the Appendix section).

ADDITIONAL **I**DEAS:

STICK-MOBILE

NEEDS: Approximately 40 popsicle sticks for every 2 people, 1 bottle of glue (Tacky Glue brand works the best - it dries faster) for each couple, a 4' long solid ramp, a box about 1' high, masking tape and a pen to mark distances, and a solid floor area at least 10' in length.

PROCEDURE: Creatively split your group into partners. If there is an extra person, a group of 3 will work. I like to do this activity after one of the "couple" ice-breakers. Supply each pair with 40 popsicle sticks and a bottle of glue. The objective for each couple is to construct an object that will travel, on its own, down a 4' ramp elevated 1' off the ground.

After giving the instructions, mingle around the room to observe interactions and progress. Set a tentative time for completion: however, adjust if more time is needed. While the groups wait for their creations to dry, have them come up with a name for the mobile, a cheer, a distance-traveled guess–anything creative to fill in the drying time. You could even move to a different activity and come back to this one.

At the launching, ask each pair to present the name of their creation. Mobiles should not be pushed down the ramp, only let go of. Be sure to launch all mobiles from the same spot and angle.

OBSERVATIONS/QUESTIONS:
- How were plans generated?
- What was it like to work with another person?
- Did you encounter any problems? How did you handle them?
- Were there any clear-cut roles in the small groups?
- Was the work shared?
- How successful do you think you were?
- Who feels responsible for the success or failure?
- Was there any sense of competition between groups?
- Were there any comments about others' mobiles?
- What reactions occurred due to the comments?

(other) •
　　　　•

VARIATIONS:
- Take turns placing popsicle sticks on the mobile.
- Have pairs come up with their own ramp.
- Add competition - see which object travels the furthest. What happens when you offer a prize?

ADDITIONAL **I**DEAS:

ROPE BUS

Thanks to Scott Trent & Clay Fiske.

NEEDS: One long activity rope (I always like old climbing rope).

PROCEDURE: When planning to move a large group from one part of a course or program to another, give them 1 long rope to hold onto. (You could even use **Trolley** rope sections–one rope between each passenger.) Have every other person holding on to opposite sides of the rope. Number off group members by 4 (or whatever small number works for you).

Tell the group they are on a bus. For the bus to move, each person should have 2 hands on the rope. Periodically the bus will stop to pick up new passengers. Start the bus up and proceed along normally for a few minutes. "Ding Ding. Bus Stop," is called. Mention there are some new passengers on the bus. When the bus starts again, the "Ones" will be walking backward. All other passengers are walking forward. The bus is off again down the trail (keep an eye on the first person). "Ding Ding. Bus Stop." There are some new passengers on the bus. When the bus starts again, the "Ones" will be walking backward and the "Twos" will be taking 2 steps forward and 1 step back. The bus is off again. "Ding Ding. Bus Stop." New passengers. "Ones" will be walking backward, "Twos" - 2 steps forward and 1 back, and "Threes" will have their eyes closed (you can provide blindfolds). And we're off. "Ding Ding"...... and "Fours" will be walking sideways with a crossover step. Off the bus goes with a "diverse" group of passengers.

Add other bus stops along the way to change walks. Be creative. The other day Clay tried 2 steps and a 1 clap. Since the bus can only go when everyone has 2 hands on the rope, a bit of problem-solving has to occur. This activity turned out to be a great process segue into diversity.

OBSERVATIONS/QUESTIONS:
- What was it like to be different?
- How did the group adapt to the changing "diversity?"
- What is diversity?
- What comments emanated from the bus? Positive? Negative?
- How was the progress of the bus? Fast? Slow?
- Did anyone get frustrated during the journey?
- Were the people on the bus taken care of? Who should be responsible for taking care of special needs?
- Were there any ideas given to make the bus ride more efficient?
- What would it be like if we were all the same?

(other) •

   •

51

VARIATIONS:
   •Other walks: Skipping, hopping (don't do this one long), Tuba Walk - 2 steps forward then stop, lift 1 knee and lean back a little, heel-toe walking.

ADDITIONAL **I**DEAS:
   •**Rope Bus** equipment can also be used with: **Birthday Rope, Raccoon Circles,** & as boundary lines.

—STICKS, STONES & BONES—
Adapted from Knapp's "Communication Patterns" activity.

NEEDS: For each pair of group members you will need 2 matching colored popsicle sticks (sticks), 2 similar small rocks or dice (stones), 2 matching dominos (bones) - any matching items will work, see variations for other ideas. You will also need an indoor or outdoor area where it is comfortable to sit down.

PROCEDURE: The only preparation part that takes a little time is coloring the sticks (I have some youth help me the night before - using markers). Make sure that every 2 sticks have the same colored patterns on them; all the sticks in the group do not have to match.

This is a good activity for understanding directions and how they can be misunderstood. When you're ready, creatively pair up group members. Give each player in the pair half of a matching set of the above gear: 1 stick, 1 stone, and 1 domino. Have the partners sit back-to-back on the ground or floor. Have each pair decide who will be the leader for the first round. The leader starts by arranging the 3 items in a pattern on the ground in front of him/herself, and then attempts to describe the arrangement to his/her partner. The partner is not allowed to speak or look around during the activity. When completed, have the partners look at each other's patterns. (If you think it is needed, ask a few questions, but don't completely process until after each player has been a leader.) Round 2, switch roles and repeat the activity. I like to time each round (about 2 minutes) to keep transitions consistent.

OBSERVATIONS/QUESTIONS:
- How did you do?
- Did the patterns turn out the same? Why or why not?
- How did leaders feel when they saw their partner's patterns?
- Where did problems arise between the two of you?
- Did you and your partner figure out a way to communicate nonverbally?
- Was it easy to follow the rules of the task?
- What would the task have been like if you could have asked questions?
- Would asking questions help you do a better job?
- How would asking questions help the leader do a better job?
- What is important about questions?
- What tends to happen if we don't ask questions when we're confused?

(other) •
          •

53

VARIATIONS:
- •If there is time, repeat the activity and allow partners to talk.
- •Add more matching objects.
- •Give each person 5 or 6 building blocks. Have the leader build and describe a sculpture.
- •A friend of mine uses larger objects with younger groups, such as a flying ring, a large softie (ball), and a Twirly. (If you don't know what Twirlies are, see "Quicksilver" by Rohnke and Butler, p. 256.)
- •If you're inside with only a paper and pencil, draw a figure on paper and have partners duplicate the drawing.
- •For the complicated corporate version, obtain 2 identical sets of building supplies - blocks, legos, cards, dominoes, marshmallows, minironis (from "50 Ways to Use Your Noodle"). Split your group in half and put them in opposite rooms. One group is the builder, one is the duplicator. Using walkie-talkies or runners, the duplicators must produce the same structure as the builders - by verbal directions only.
- •Try this one (almost impossible). Invest in one of those new fancy lego structures, one of the small ones like a small bug or car. Now give all the pieces to one group and have another group give verbal directions from behind a barrier (blanket or cubical wall) based on the picture shown on the box!!
- •Stand in rows of 5 or 6. The first person in the front of the line will need a piece of paper and a wide tip marker. The group facilitator will draw a simple structure on her own sheet of paper - like a large cat, some geometric shapes, or a house with windows and a cloud floating by. The facilitator, with picture in hand, stands in the back of all the groups and asks the last person in each line to turn around (no one else should turn around) and view the picture. When these players are ready, they turn around and draw the picture they saw on the backs of the person in front of them - using their index fingers. Each player in turn draws what they felt on the next player. The first person in line draws on the paper. Compare the drawings. What is the end result of this communication? What would the result be if each person at the end of each line had a copy of the same picture and everyone did their drawing at the same time? Would they all be on the same page? Or would it be the same back?

ADDITIONAL **I**DEAS:

Thanks to Lenny Diamond.

NEEDS: A paper roll segment for each member of the group (see Note), 1 marble, a small receptacle, and any type of area (inside an area involving furniture would be interesting).

Note: Paper rolls - TP, paper towel, wrapping paper rolls. You can cut these down the side pretty easily to form straight or spiral gutter shapes. Also, you can leave them whole to pass the marble through. A blind faith type of activity.

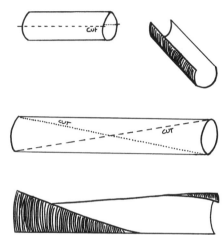

PROCEDURE: The objective of the activity is for the group to devise a method for moving a marble through a series of the hand-held paper gutters and then successfully drop the marble into a receptacle located 20' to 50' away (depending on size of the group) as quickly as possible. Here are the guidelines described by Lenny:
  •Paper gutters cannot touch each other or the ground.
  •Player controlling a marble cannot move his/her feet.
  •No one can move arms beyond the width of his or her body space.
  •Only the first person can touch the marble.
  •Marble must not move backward.
  •Receptacle cannot be moved.
  •Any violation of above guidelines or if the marble drops, start over.
Provide the amount of paper gutters you would like the group to use in a big bag or box and let them get to it.

I tried this activity with a church group. I told them the marble was their faith, and they each had to take care of how they received, carried, and passed their faith. I had them all sitting on the **Quad Jam** element, and they couldn't get up off the wood. They solved the problem of getting the marble around by giving up their paper gutter to others and then getting it back to finish the travels. Compromise at its best.

Andy Greif, who turned me onto this great activity, says he likes to give each player a marble to take home as an "anchor" for the experience. He also suggested giving out wooden marbles - each player can write a strength he or she contributed onto the marble. Thanks Andy!

OBSERVATIONS/**Q**UESTIONS:
- How did you contribute to the activity?
- What roles were assumed during the activity?
- How did you decide on gutter pieces? Did everyone agree?
- How was the first person chosen(the toucher of the marble)?
- Did anyone else want to be the first person? Why?
- What was the group reaction to dropping the marble?
- What type of problem-solving went on?

(other) •

    •

VARIATIONS:
- Lenny's original format called for PVC pipe sections cut down the middle so you have a "gutter" type piece of equipment. This is the best of all possible worlds. However, I had a hard time finding the equipment and then a person that could perform the task. So I went to foam (keep reading).
- My favorite variation to date is using the wooden marbles. Have each person write their name on the wooden marble. Then send the "person" through the system. VERY interesting dynamics.
- Try passing the marbles up a flight of stairs or the incline of a hill. (Thanks, Jim Cain.)
- More than one gutter per person - let the group allocate pieces.
- More than one marble.
- Place a time limit on the task (one minute from start to finish).
- Non-verbal; one handed; several members blindfolded.
- Foam pipe insulation, 7/8" diameter, works well too - found at any hardware store. Find different shapes, like corners, if you can. Cut the insulation in half (there is usually a half separation in it already) to expose the groove inside. This is where the marble will travel. Cut a number of different lengths for participants. Players like to squeeze the foam around the marble during this one. You can let them, or not.
- Another resource that works very well - 90 degree interior plastic corner molding. This stuff is very easy to cut into any length you want.
- You could also use the PVC sections of **The Cube** element for an interesting variation.
- If you're REALLY into all these variations, pick up a copy of "50 Ways to Use Your Noodle," and try Immobile Chopsticks - lots of fun.

ADDITIONAL **I**DEAS:
- **Pipeline** equipment can also be used with: **Marble Movers**.

NEEDS: Four pieces of plywood (1' x 2' in size), a bunch of bandannas and an expanse about 40' wide. (The boards should work out to 1 for every 4 players with one extra board for the group to work with.)

PROCEDURE: I have a favorite story for this one.

> "You are all inhabitants of a beautiful paradise island. Unfortunately, your island has an active volcano on it about to explode and cover the island with lava. Since you never had a reason to leave your island, you do not have any large boats; however, you do have small fishing rafts. You know of a neighboring island that is safe from your island's destruction. As best you can tell, there are only five minutes (see text below) until eruption. Anyone left on the island after that time is soon to perish. The only concerns you may have during your crossing are the blinding needle fish in the water. Anyone that steps into the water will need a protective bandage to cover their eyes from the sun until they reach the other island for special medicine. Take care on your travels and do not throw your rafts because they could be destroyed."

I ask for any questions at this point before I start the time. I set the time at 5 minutes to force them to cross the expanse together. (If there is unlimited time, two or three go, then one comes back, and two more go and so on. Low teamwork concept here.)

I also like to put obstacles in the water area; things the group has to go around. It makes for interesting dynamics.

You can choose to blindfold or not. I blindfold any water touchers. I may also adapt the story and add "paralyzing puffer fish." The ones that paralyze a hand if it touches the water (ground). This switches around workers and sometimes changes leadership roles.

Safety Note: Do not allow the boards to be thrown!

OBSERVATIONS/QUESTIONS:
- Who took a leadership role in the activity?
- How many players were able to share ideas? Was everyone heard?
- What kind of plan, if any, was generated?
- Did the group work together or in fragments?
- Which individuals composed the small group fragments?
- Was anyone left back on the island? What were the feelings about that?
- Did the people left on the island speak up at all about their situation?

•What was it like to be on the rafts together?
•How were blindfolded players taken care of? Who took care of them?
•Was the work shared during the trip?
•How did the group react to making it across together?

(other) •

      •

VARIATIONS:

•Bring along extra gear to cramp the space on the boards (e.g., day packs, water buckets, boxes).
•Use the 4' sections of **Trolley** rope instead of the boards. Require feet to be touching a rope if a player's foot is on the ground. Very low cost initiative - and very portable too!
•You could use the Boxes (see **Rooftops**) from the elements section to simulate the famous, Hot Chocolate River activity (if you know this one). However, you will need spotting during this elevated traverse.

ADDITIONAL IDEAS:

•**Islands** equipment can also be used with: **Mine Field, Block Hop,** & **Box Top**.

MARBLE MOVERS

Adapted from Jackie Gerstein, "The Family Circuit" Newsletter.

NEEDS: A "Marble Mover" for each group member (a 3' long 1/4" dowel with a plastic spoon taped to one end and a tape mark all the way around the dowel 3" from the other end), a mid-size plastic cup for every player, and a Frisbee type container (you will need a low lip edge for this one). I usually put in about 5 marbles for each player in the container (but I don't tell them this).

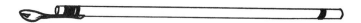

PROCEDURE: Place the container of marbles on the ground or floor. Have the players sit Indian Style in a circle around the container at a distance to where they can just reach the vessel with their Marble Mover. They must stay in their spot throughout the activity. Have each player place his or her cup next to the hip of the side from which they will be holding the Marble Mover (i.e., If they are using their left hand, the cup goes a few inches from their left hip.) Tell the group, "The goal is for each person to get as many marbles as they can in their cup. You can use only one hand to hold the Marble Mover, and that one hand must remain behind the tape mark at the opposite end from the spoon at all times. The task is complete when all the marbles in the container are gone."

The objective in my head has to do with the group sharing the marbles evenly. It will be very difficult for each player to drop marbles in their own cup. But they surely will try - especially true with the younger groups I have worked with. It has often taken them the longest to figure out the sharing concept. However, there have been the exceptions on both ends of the generation gap.

OBSERVATIONS/QUESTIONS:
- Who won?
- Who realized the need to help each other?
- Was it hard to accept help from other people? Why?
- What were some problems you encountered as you tried to help?
- How did you work through the problems?
- Did everyone feel they received their fair share?
- Was there a plan for equality?
- Who had to speak up to receive their share?
- Is it important to be fair? Why?
- Was anyone hurt in any way during the activity?
- Why is it important to keep each other safe?

(other) •
       •

VARIATION:
- Tape a fork to the dowel rod, place the marbles on the floor. I call this one "Fork-Um."

ORIGINAL **V**ERSION:

Jackie Gerstein has called this activity "Nurturing Spoons." Instead of marbles, she uses a food substance. She has suggested icecream, her favorite on warm days. The same idea goes, the group would hopefully realize that they must feed each other to be successful. Be aware of any inappropriate feeding techniques. When the feeding frenzy takes over, make sure the same spoon goes into the same mouth each time. **Be safe.** Shoving the spoon in another person's mouth should be avoided! When I play (I like to use M & Ms) I always have another staff member help me watch the group.

Jackie also likes to use this story along with her activity:

"A person was struggling to understand the difference between happiness and sadness. He asked for a guide to help him. A guide appeared and said, 'I will help you. I will take you on two journeys.' On the first journey they arrived at a place where a great number of people were seated around a large table. They were all very thin and looked near death. There was a large bowl of porridge in the center of the table. They were trying to eat but could not feed themselves because the spoons were longer than their arms, and they could not put the food into their own mouths. The guide said, 'This is sadness.' For their second journey, they arrived at a place where a great number of people were seated around a large table. They looked well and happy. There was a large bowl of porridge in the middle of the table. These people were using the same spoons, the ones too long to reach into their own mouth. The difference was, they were feeding one another. The guide said, 'This is happiness.'"

ADDITIONAL **I**DEAS:
- **Marble Movers** equipment can also be used with: **Tosser Touch, Pipeline** & **It**.

THE GREAT EGG DROP
Thanks to Karl Rohnke, "The Bottomless Bag Again."

NEEDS: Each group of 2 players will need 20 straws, 30" of 1/2" masking tape and a raw egg (still in the shell). You will also need a bunch of old newspapers for the drop zone and a stepladder or chair.

PROCEDURE: The task is to design a delivery system that will protect a raw egg, dropped from a predetermined height, using only the straws and the tape provided.

Creatively divide your group into partners, a group of 3 is fine if there is an extra person. Give groups 20 minutes to design, construct and plan a promotional pitch to highlight the name and benefits of their protective delivery system.

After the work time, gather together for the dropping. If time allows, I like to start at a lower level drop and work my way up to higher drops. This gives a bit of a chance for all eggs to survive at least one fall. Don't forget to provide time for promotional pitches. Bombs Away!

OBSERVATIONS/QUESTIONS:
- How did you agree upon a design?
- Did each person contribute equally to the project?
- Who came up with the name?..the benefits?
- Was it difficult to speak in front of the group?
- What were your expectations of the device?
- Did you plan for failure or success? What happened?
- How did it feel to succeed?..fail?
- Did you use all the time available? Do you think it was a factor?
- Was there any competition going on?
- What was the most important part of this activity?

(other) •
   •

VARIATIONS:

- •Write each person's name on the egg. Now it's your team and not just an egg that must survive.
- •Which pair can use the least amount of materials to survive the drop.
- •Here's a great "object drop" initiative from Glen Olsen via Sam Sikes (from his "Executive Marbles" book). Provide these resources to every pair of players: 4 sheets of 8 1/2" x 11" paper, 4 paper clips, 2' of masking tape, scissors (optional), and you'll want a stop watch for timing the drops. The challenge - construct a contraption that, when dropped 8', will take the <u>longest</u> time to reach the ground. It must free-fall and be self-contained (no other resources attached). Give each pair 3 drops to get the best time.

ADDITIONAL IDEAS:

NEEDS: An 8' bungee cord with end-hooks or rope and 2 tamper poles. (A tamper can be found at a large hardware store. It has a square metal base with a long handle. Place a 2" x 6' length of PVC piping over the handle and you have a tamper pole. These poles may have to be guyed down for support. I like to tie the guys to gallon jugs of water. Use large hose clamps as pipe attachments for the guy ropes (see diagram.)

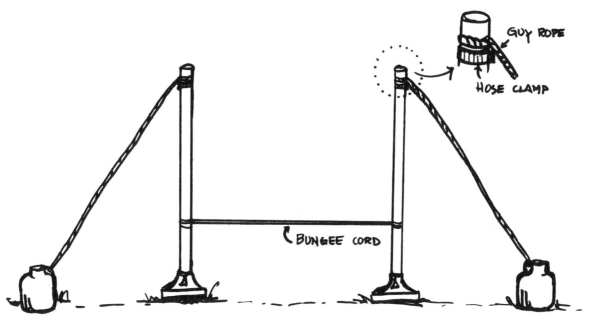

Place the tamper poles about 7' apart. Wrap the cord around the PVC pipe a couple of times and hook it back to itself. Set the cord or rope height at the inseam height of the tallest person in the group.

PROCEDURE: Holding hands in a line, at all times, the group must go over the cord stretched between two sturdy points without touching it. If someone touches or breaks a hand hold, the entire group starts over.

FACILITATION/SAFETY:
•Ensure that the anchor points are stable.
•Check bungee cord for any damage. Check connection devices.
•The group should call touches.
•Present the problem and answer questions before the group begins.

This is a relatively safe activity. Spot any lifting that occurs. Caution groups about hand grip, it should be comfortable. Permit them to change grip if there is a problem. (You could also have players hold a bandanna between them to provide a good rotation point.) Caution them about where their feet are going to land to avoid twisting ankles. Keep this one slow and controlled.

OBSERVATIONS/QUESTIONS:
•Where did the leadership come from?
•How was the group order determined? Who participated in the decision?
•Did ability (or gender) play a part in the order?
•Why was the cord height set the way it was? Was it fair?
•What was the reaction to a touch? What was a touch to the group?
•How was the group supporting each other?
•What type of communication was going on?

(other) •

•

VARIATIONS:
•Have the group members hold hands in a circle.
•Blindfold touchers.
•Blindfold all but the first and last group members.
•Adjust the cord and have them go under - only feet can touch the ground.
•Use masking tape instead of cord.
•Set the tamper poles closer together. Spotting is very important here.

ADDITIONAL IDEAS:
•**Electric Amoeba** equipment can also be used with: **Leakers, Descend-sion, Mine Field, Blind Beam, Electric Porthole,** & **The Web**.

TANGLES

HISTORY: I feel the need to present a little historical capsule on this activity. **Tangles** is my interpretation of the "Human Knot" which dates back to German dancing (I think?). Anyway, this one gets them "together."

NEEDS: Medium-size area (bandanna for each person - for variation below).

PROCEDURE: You might want to try this activity first in smaller groups. Then combine the groups (of 12 if you feel lucky) once they understand the concept.

Standing in a circle facing in, grab hands with the players next to you. Starting with one person, have him send a pulse around the circle by gently squeezing the hand of one of the group members next to him. When that group member feels her hand being squeezed, she gently squeezes the hand of the next person, and so on until it gets back to the starting squeezer. This system is needed to check for a circle in the Knot a bit later - stick with me.

Now drop hands and then have everyone in the circle put their right hand into the middle and grab the hand of a player who is not standing next to them. If there is an extra hand it will be used up in a second. Next, have everyone put their left hand in the circle. Again, don't have them grab the person's hand standing next to them or the person they are already holding onto. Join up the extra right hand here (if there is one). Now, have a person start a pulse like they practiced - this is to check if the result of un-tangling will be a circle. The key is for everyone to get and send a pulse. If this does not occur, have everyone let go, and regrab hands again following the same procedure as above. When hands are connected and everyone sends and receives a pulse, try to untangle the group back into a circle.

Allow people to readjust hand grips to make it easy (this is where players could hold onto a bandanna, it serves as a pivot point). Make sure you check in with players who look uncomfortable to see if they need to adjust something.

Patience is a major key here. You might frontload the activity with some goal setting. Would the group like to use some breaks and regrasps? Does the group want a leader outside the group (unattached) to help solve the tangles? How long does the group want to spend, or how long does the group have for the activity?

OBSERVATIONS/QUESTIONS:
  • What was it like being so close together?
  • How did people contribute to the group?

65

•Who took a leadership role?
•Did anyone offer suggestions that didn't get heard? What did you do?
•Did anyone get frustrated? What did you do about it?
•What was it like to wait while others were active?
•What did it take to be successful?
•Did you use the one break? Was that okay with everyone?
•Is it all right to be unsuccessful?
•What can you learn from this activity?

(other) •

•

VARIATIONS:

•Here's a great lead-in activity from Laurie Frank (co-author with me on, "Games for Teachers"), **A Very Big Knot**. With everyone standing in a big circle facing in, have players cross their arms in front of their bodies so the left hand is reaching past their right shoulder and the right hand past their left shoulder. Everyone holds hands with the players next to them (adding the bandannas here is a good idea). Now, the objective is to untie the very large knot without letting go, with all players facing <u>in</u> toward the center. (I like this one.) Once the players are facing in, ask them if they want a more difficult challenge. Move into **Tangles**.
•Blindfold a few players part of the way through the activity.
•Everyone wear a helmet (it would be an interesting picture?)
•With larger groups, give them a section of 4' **Trolley** rope to connect with each other. This produces a very interesting spider web pattern within the center of the group for all to see and problem solve. I like to use this variation with groups that are not very comfortable holding hands, or maybe should not be holding hands.
•Add a large beach ball to the center of the knot, and tell the group the ball can't touch the ground during the process.

ADDITIONAL IDEAS:

NEEDS: The more players, the larger the area should be (make sure the area is free of obstructions).

PROCEDURE: (An oldie but a goodie.) Form a shoulder-to-shoulder circle with the group. Ask them to turn their left shoulders into the center of the circle (90 degree turn). From this point, players move toward the center of the circle until everyone is touching the heels of the person in front of them with their own toes - this may not always be physically possible, so get them as close as you can. (Make sure the group is in a circle shape at this point - this is very important.) The objective from here will be to SLOWLY sit down together until everyone is sitting on the lap behind them.

As the facilitator, you must direct the sitting movement. It is best to have each person grab the upper arms (around the biceps) of the person in front of them - not the top of the shoulder. This way everyone can help each other stand up if needed. Keep the action slow and controlled. There will be a "butterflies in the stomach zone" where individuals may panic - usually right before each player reaches the knees of the person behind him or her. Warn the group about this. Encourage them to move past that point. There may be some falling at first - just be as careful as you can, then try again.

Get up together after a successful sit, holding the upper arms of the person in front of them. I often use this activity to close out a session. It is one that they like to talk about.

OBSERVATIONS/**Q**UESTIONS:
   •What was the activity like?
   •Was anyone skeptical about the success of the stacking?
   •Who felt the danger zone? What was it like?
   •How many ways did you support each other?
   •What happened when one part of the circle had difficulty?
   •How does that relate to life in the Real World?
(other) •
         •

VARIATIONS:
- Lead a little walking while the group is sitting in laps. Call out "Left" and "Right" slowly, e.g. "1, 2, 3, left, 1, 2, 3, right." It does work!
- Start one person in a chair and stack from there (that rhymes).

ADDITIONAL **I**DEAS:

—WATERFALL

Thanks to Joel Cryer via Tim Reed via Sam Sikes,
"Executive Marbles and Other Team Building Activities."

NEEDS: (For the Chris Cavert variation.) One bandanna and one mid-size paper cup for every 2 players in the group. A large tub filled with water (or other water source - a lake?). One good size bucket that will hold water. A measuring cup or water bottle with measure markings. A couple of boundary markers - I use 2 of my old climbing/activity ropes. Cones are good too.

PROCEDURE: This is a "get wet" activity, so be prepared (or use the indoor version described in the Variations below). You'll have to do a little set-up first. The over-all idea behind **Waterfall** will be to move water from one place to another. So, set up a "loading" zone area for the main water supply. Set boundaries around or near the water supply big enough for the entire group to stand in - if they choose to do this. The "unloading" zone is where the water will be taken. The farther away this zone is, the more challenging the activity will be. Set the un-loading zone bucket in the center of a boundary area smaller than the loading zone - so the entire group <u>cannot</u> fit in. Having a few obstacles between the loading and unloading zone also makes the adventure interesting. You're ready to play.

Split your group up into pairs (if there is an extra person, form one group of 3 - makes for another interesting process). Give each pair a bandanna and one cup. Use a fun story to explain why you have to move the water from the loading zone to the unloading zone. While the group is within either zone, they may touch the cup; however, once they leave the zone, the cup of water must be carried on an outstretched bandanna. At no time between zones may the cup be touched in any way including through the bandanna. If the cup drops, a player may pick up the cup and take it back to the loading zone for a refill. Give the group a time limit - 5 minutes has worked well for me. After the time is up, measure the water they transferred to the unloading zone. Do some processing about the process. After some problem-solving, see if the group would like to try and move more water with a second attempt. You could goal set - how much water can they move?

I have had some interesting processing with this one. Most of the younger groups

I have used this with get stuck in the assumption that they are working in pairs and cannot help other team members in getting the cup of water on the out-stretched bandanna. If there is a group of 5, how might they work together? How does this small group affect the large group? I've seen some of the "older" kids' groups think out of the box, but...

OBSERVATIONS/QUESTIONS:

- What were some overall observations of the activity? What happened?
- What sort of communication went on before the water started moving?
- How did partners communicate?
- What was the frustration level during the moving?
- Did anyone come up with a plan to help move more water?
- Did anyone have a plan they didn't share? Why?
- Did anyone ask for help?
- What worked well for you?..the group as a whole?
- What didn't work so well?
- If you were to do it again, what would make the process more productive?

(other) •

- •

VARIATIONS:

- The via,via Sam Sikes version. In small groups of 3 to 8, have them take hold of a bandanna by the edges so that everyone has both hands on it. Pull it taut and make it flat. "I will place a cup of water in the middle of the bandanna. You may not let go of the bandanna. The edges of the bandanna must always be below the top of the cup. Without spilling any water or letting go of the bandanna, follow me. Should you spill any water, we will start over." Move slowly so that the group can keep up with you. Make obstacles comparable to the group's ability. Finish the exercise by asking the team to place the bandanna and cup on the floor.
- For the non-wet version, fill the cup with beans. As Sam says, "Nobody likes to spill the beans."

ADDITIONAL IDEAS:

CORPORATE BOX

Thanks to the 1996 Activity Colloquium, Tulsa, Oklahoma.

NEEDS: One rope about 75' long, 8 - 14" carpet squares (you could also use 8 boxes from **Roof Tops**), and 2 hula hoops or rings made of rope (**Raccoon Circles** would work nicely).

PROCEDURE: Set up the playing area as diagrammed below. The boundaries are in a rectangle shape, but a square could be used. (A rectangle shape will bring up issues of fairness if this is a program goal.)

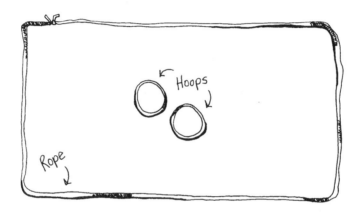

This activity can be done with small or large groups. Split the group into 4 smaller teams (but they are still one group), each standing outside one side of the boundary area. Give each group 2 carpet squares. The objective is for the groups on opposite sides to exchange places, as quickly as possible, without stepping on the floor or ground when inside the rectangle. Here are the other parameters:

1) The boundary area and rings inside may not be moved in any way.
2) No more than 3 feet may be on any square at one time.
3) The rings inside the area are safe zones (you can step inside them) but once utilized, they must <u>always</u> be occupied by 2 people within a reasonable amount of time (someone must be stepping into it as someone is stepping out) or the ring is lost.
4) Loss of human contact with a square results in the loss of the square. Any momentary loss of contact, the resource take away the resource.
5) You may not enter the rectangle from any other side than the one you started on.
6) You may only exit the opposite side from where you started.
7) You may not "scoot" or "ski" across the rectangle.
8) No jumping - an unsafe process.
9) Squares cannot be thrown - unsafe, plus it violates rule #4.
10) If anyone fails to follow any of the parameters, they must go back to their starting side.

With all that said and done, what is the concept? The hidden agenda has to deal with sharing resources. If all the teams would share their resources and create a diagonal line - as a group, from one corner across to another (making two triangles) - switching sides would go much faster. In most cases that I have seen, it has been "all teams for themselves." After losing resources some teams will figure out the sharing concept, or at least help another team. In any case, it has always been very interesting to watch.

The group may get to a point where they can no longer move. What are the options? If they ask to start again, they must tell me one thing they will do differently on the next try.

I have written the above variation, to allow for more success for smaller groups - masking the sharing idea a little more. See Variations below for other ideas.

OBSERVATIONS/QUESTIONS:
- What sort of planning took place?..by small group?..by large group?
- Was there any sharing of ideas? Any copying?
- Is copying good?..bad?..cheating?
- What was the reaction over losing a resource? Who was blamed?
- How did groups "regroup" after losing resources?
- Were you working together?
- Who gave you the rules of the game? Did you accept them? Did you ever try to challenge them? Did you ever ask to change any of the rules? How would changing the rules affect the activity?
- Is there a way you could all work together to be more successful - if success was measured by a better time?
- What are some keys to becoming more successful?
- What is the overall reaction to the processes you were involved in?

(other) •

•

VARIATIONS: (As suggested in the original text, there are a few ways to force the sharing idea a little faster if desired.)
- Change rule #2 above to read: "No more than 2 feet may be on any square at one time."
- Add this as rule #11 - You may not contact or use the same square twice in succession. Once you lose contact with a square or have used the square, someone else must be in contact with it *before* you may come into contact

with it again. Define "use a square" - it means to make progress toward your goal.

·Use only 7 total squares. Give 2 squares to 3 sides and only 1 to the 4th - don't say anything about the unequal distribution.

ADDITIONAL **I**DEAS:

·Make a sheet of rules for the group, hand it to them. Make them the experts.
·**Corporate Box** equipment can also be used with: **Birthday Rope, Rope Bus, Lily Pads & Islands,** & **Block Hop**.

Noodles? (This does not involve pasta of any kind!) Noodles are those foam pool toys. Sam Sikes and I wrote a book called, "50 Ways to Use Your Noodle: Loads of Land Games With Foam Noodle Toys." The book contains 30 games and 20 problem-solving activities. I thought I'd throw a couple of promotional activities in here to peak your interest. (Details on how to get the book are included in the Resources section.)

NEEDS: You'll need some Noodles. Most Noodles are sold 64" long and about 3" in diameter - we call these "maxaronis." For these initiatives, you'll need one "midaroni," or half a maxaroni, for each player. (Cut the "max" in half with a serrated knife – spotting required!)

3-D NOODLE SHAPES ──────────────

PROCEDURE: This is a spin off of the blind geometric shapes groups will make with a long rope. Let's go 3-D. Give each member of your group a bandanna. After they place them over their eyes, put out the number of Noodles you need to make the shape: Cube = 12 or 24; three-sided pyramid = 6, 12, or 24; four-sided pyramid = 8 or 16 noodles. First the group has to find the noodles, then make the shape. To add a little more challenge, ask them to hold the shape up off the ground.

DNA ──────────────

PROCEDURE: Have the players face inward, holding Midaronis between their open palms around a complete circle. Now by moving slowly, have the circle stretch outward until the largest size is reached without dropping any noodles. Remember, only the palms should be touching the noodle. This will encourage communication between participants as they reach their limits. Then shrink the circle to the smallest size, and finally return the circle to the original size.

When the group is ready to increase the challenge, turn the circle inside out without out dropping any noodles. We will let groups try this option any way they can - usually meaning they can touch the noodles with their fingers. When the circle is inverted, ask them to return to the original circle, but this time do not allow fingers to grab the noodle.

NOODLE WALK I

PROCEDURE: The group must travel from point A to point B without the noodles breaking their connection with one another.

SCENARIO: "You are a group of specialists gathered together to dispose of some toxic waste containers discovered by some vacationers back in the woodlands of a small island off the coast of Florida. Only 2 containers are leaking from one end, the rest are leaking from both ends. To contain the leaks, the ends of each container must be pressed against each other during transportation. If at any time during transportation a specialists' container becomes disconnected from another container, that specialist must reconnect with a different container (reconnecting with the same container may cause oxomorphi-creboification resulting in accelerated toxic leakage). Containers may never be reconnected to each other once they have been disconnected (e.g., if container #3 disconnects from container #2, these two cannot be reconnected in that order). Also, to prevent any subcutaneous skin damage, specialists may not hold directly over the connecting points of the containers. Your leakage expert will be available for any consultations on disconnection during transportation."

The scenario covers most of the ground rules. The group should be allowed to figure out the additional limitations (like the noodles with one end leaking will be at the front and back ends of the line).

Another stipulation added for high functioning groups would be to disallow any contact with noodles other than the specialists' own (you can't physically touch any other noodle but the one you start with).

OBSERVATION/QUESTIONS: (I'm going to let you run with these.)

ADDITIONAL IDEAS: If you buy the book, you'll get 47 more!!
  •Use noodles in your **Mine Field** and for tag games.

NEEDS: One hula-hoop for every 4 players and 1 extra hoop (small groups could be divided in 3's). One 8 1/2" x 11" piece of paper for each player and some markers.

The set up is important. The hula-hoops are set up like a clock (see diagram - if you have 12 groups you are set! - but if you don't, you'll figure it out). Place the extra hoop in the middle, then set the other hoops 5 good-size steps away from the center hoop with an equal distance between them around the circumference of the clock shape - that's 1 big step for each person in the small group, plus 1 extra step. Adjust for smaller group size - keep in mind the action that will be taking place during the activity - group members will be stepping on their paper (you hope). If you are working on a slick floor, don't make the steps too far apart - the paper may slip

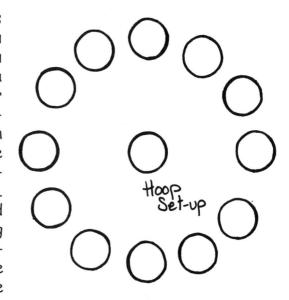

Hoop Set-up

out from under a long step. Now, if the group members tend to set them out too far, you will have to deal with the safety of this when it happens (because you're not going to tell them they cannot do this during the directions). Well, you might have to read this a few times but it's worth it. (If you're a visual person, get a bunch of people together, have a conference, and I'll visit!)

PROCEDURE: Gather together in teams of 4 for this one (be creative with left-overs - my mom always said). Give each player a sheet of paper and have them write their name on it - real big. (If I have planned to use this activity, I will have each person put their name on a sheet of paper as they arrive. Just before the activity I might add this little initiative, "How long do you think it will take to get everyone their sheet of paper from this pile?") With paper in hand, ask each "team" to position themselves by a hula-hoop so you can give instructions.

My intention for this activity (but I don't tell them outright) is for players, in small groups, to start in one of the perimeter hoops, using their sheets of paper to step on as they travel to the center hoop. After stepping inside the center hoop, each player must find another hoop to stand in - excluding their original and center hoop - without touching the ground. If at any time someone touches the ground, that player must return to his/her original hoop to start again. To tell them all of this would be too easy for an adventure. So to add a bit of a twist I give each small group a copy of the following rhyme:

> "All in your group will start inside a hoop.
> To be fleet of feet, you must use your sheet.
> Each must make a loop touching the space in the center hoop.
> A new place you must find to end your journey, to unwind.
> If any open ground you touch, return to your starting space.
> Please take care in your travels, for surely this is not a race."

In this way the players become the experts. It's also interesting to watch what happens to this information during the activity. If I'm working with a Corporate group, I'll call the directions their "Standard Operating Procedures." Again, watch what happens to the SOPs during the activity.

Presenting the introduction notice I used the words "team" and "group." What do you think will happen? Will the group work together or separate into teams?

Also, I often use this one close to, if not at, the end of a program. My hope with this activity is that each person will leave their paper (themselves) at the disposal of the group - leave it on the ground in a path to the center. All groups must have a "center," a place of reference. And it takes each member of that group to support that place (I'm rambling). You would be surprised at what happens, especially when someone has their name on something - interesting.

OBSERVATIONS/QUESTIONS:
- Describe the actions of your team during the activity.
- Describe some actions of the group during the activity.
- How were the papers handled? Were there possession issues?
- Evaluate the role of the player with the directions/SOPs.
- What are the benefits of directions/SOPs?
- How well were the directions/SOPs followed?
- Describe some conflicting interpretations of the directions/SOPs.
- How were these conflicts resolved?
- What is the difference between a group and a team?
- What was the end result of the group activity?

(other) •
   •

VARIATIONS:
- •Give out only 1 rhyme sheet for the entire group. (This is very interesting.)
- •Give out 1 line of the rhyme to 6 different players in the group.

ADDITIONAL **I**DEAS:
- • **Chris-Cross** equipment can also be used with: **Boundary Ball, Lily Pads & Islands, Corporate Box, Mine Field,** & **Electric Porthole**.

LEAKERS

Thanks to Madeline Constantine,
Program Coordinator, Stony Acres East Stroudsburg University,
East Stroudsburg, Pennsylvania.

NEEDS: First you'll need 2 Leaker Tubes. These are made with the Tamper pole PVC pipes (see **Electric Amoeba** for description). Drill 1/4" holes, about 20 to 30 of them, evenly around and up and down through the PVC pipes. You have "Leaker Tubes." To make the activity easier, buy a rubber PVC cap that fits the size PVC pipe you have. The caps I have come with a hose clamp on them - you push the cap onto one end and tighten the clamp. You can also be creative (and more challenging) by not providing the cap. Other needs - 2 Ping-Pong balls, 3 plastic cups, and a source of water.

PROCEDURE: Divide the group you have into 2 equal teams (but remember they are still a group). Ask a member of each team to hold up a tube (one for each team), vertically with the capped end down. Place a Ping-Pong ball in the open end of each tube and then ask the "group" to get the Ping-Pong balls out of the tubes without moving the tubes toward a horizontal direction (they can't pick up the tube and spill out the PPBs).

The 3 cups will be lying near the tubes. With a bit of willpower, the group should find a use for the cups - water down the tubes. Of course the participants will have to plug the holes somehow. And what's with the uneven amount of cups? All the more fun to play with, my dear! Also, you will have to consider the activewear the players will be donning, because there is a wet factor here.

OBSERVATIONS/QUESTIONS:
   •What kinds of ideas were shared for solving the problem?
   •Did everyone have a chance to share their idea? Is this important?
   •What about the cups?
   •What situations (problems) did you run into as the activity progressed?
    How were they solved (if at all)?
   •What went on between the 2 "teams"?
   •Who decided the activity was competitive?
   •What sorts of competition were you regularly involved in outside of the
    program? Are these good or bad?
   •What was the reaction to getting wet? Then what?
(other) •
      •

VARIATIONS:
- •Cain & Jolliff (1998) have some fun "Tube & Water" activities. You can use the PVC tubes from **The Cube** activity and do **Pipeline** with water (found in this section). A great way to cool off on a hot day.

ADDITIONAL **I**DEAS:
- • **Leakers** equipment can also be used with: **Pipeline** & **Descend-sion**.

THE TUNNEL

NEEDS: One 8' x 20' tarp, sewn into a tunnel. I prefer a tarp that has a length of rope sewn into the seam. For a class act tunnel, I set hole grommets 2" apart down the 20' sides (yes, this is a lot of work, but this way lasts the longest). Sew the 20' sides together, either through the hole grommets with thick string or by using thin, nylon string and a large needle; now you have a tunnel.

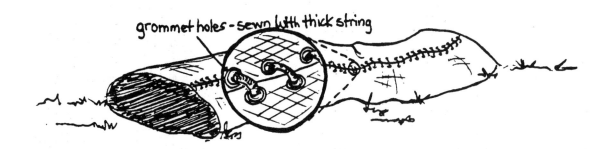

grommet holes - sewn with thick string

PROCEDURE: Divide the group in half. One half of the group stands at each end of the tunnel. How fast can the group switch places with the other half of the group by going through the tunnel. Each time one person goes into the tunnel, a person from the other group must go into the tunnel.

FACILITATION/SAFETY:
- Remind participants to pass others carefully inside the tunnel.
- Present the problem and answer questions before the group begins.

This is a straight forward element. Watch for silliness and inappropriate behavior while individuals are in the tunnel.

After the group has gone through once, I have them do a bit of problem-solving and attempt the activity again, trying to beat the time set. After they have beaten their record, I present different challenges: Try the same activity with a large balloon between your teeth; take a large beach ball with you; take along a cup of water to fill a container at each end of the tunnel (this one always has great sounds emanating from within the tunnel); fill up the tunnel with bodies - then call someone out; or any other idea that might present a challenge.

OBSERVATIONS/QUESTIONS:
- What sort of planning took place? Did the group plan together as a whole, or did they plan separately in their small groups?
- What was it like to go through the tunnel? Did anyone become uncomfortable?

•How were you able to beat the set record? What prevented you from beating the record?
•What was difficult about the activity? How did you overcome the difficulty?
•What reactions arose as participants went through the challenges?
•What did you learn about yourself during this activity?

(other) •

•

VARIATIONS:

ADDITIONAL **I**DEAS:

HOLE-IN-ONE

Thanks to Madeline Constantine,
Program Coordinator, Stony Acres East Stroudsburg University,
East Stroudsburg, Pennsylvania.

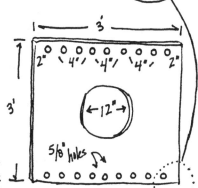

NEEDS: 9" to 12" diameter ball. 3' x 3' board with a hole large enough for the ball to fall through (the hole can be on or off center). Holes are drilled on 2 opposing sides of the board for ropes or string to fit through (see diagram). One 4' string or rope for each person (I use the ropes from the **Trolleys** element). One container for the ball to be dropped into. Blindfolds for the challenge variation.

PROCEDURE: Place the ropes, with one end knotted, through the holes near the sides. Set the ball on the ground near the board. Tell the group that the ball must be transported from point A to point B, located approximately 20-30 yards away, without rolling off the board, touching the string/rope, or falling through the hole between points (basically, the ball may only touch or be touched by the wood). The ball is then deposited into the receptacle.

(Include goal setting as an objectives of this activity by asking the group to come up with a number of "touches" they believe it will take to achieve their outcome. A touch would include human touch, the ball touching a string/rope, or the ball touching the ground. This will add another dynamic to the planning process.)

<u>Additional Guidelines</u>
•Players must hold the ropes at the ends without any wrapping.
•The ball can only be touched by a player in order to start over if dropped.
•All members of the group must participate.

(There are many ways to "set up" this activity. My favorite has the group working together, but each individual has their own "end" to keep up in order for the group to succeed. From here I let them go ahead and try the activity. They soon find out it takes a lot more than individual efforts to be successful with this one.)

Madeline shares a "Typical Frontload Scenario" one might use with an adult Work Team. "You have explained to me that back at work there are times when 'point' team members need to take the lead to complete a project. The remaining 'support' members need to be peripherally involved, trusting that the task will be coordinated by others. This exercise will give your team an opportunity to explore how members communicate in these situations."

(In the scenario above you could appoint a leader or leaders to instruct the players on the use of the strings/ropes during the activity. Players can only do what they are told. Not an easy task.)

OBSERVATIONS/QUESTIONS:
- Why was the task completed or not completed? (Madeline)
- What was your roll in the activity?
- What sort of planning took place before the first attempt? How did this change as you went along?
- How was communication between the leaders and the players?
- Were you able to meet your goals? Why? Why not?
- How did the equipment affect the process? What did you do about it?
- What would make this activity easier?
- If you were to do this again, what would you do differently?
- What sort of leadership would be easiest to follow for this activity?

(other) •
•

VARIATIONS:
- Set all the resources down and then ask the group to "construct" an apparatus that will transport the ball. All other guidelines apply to crossing (i.e., secure string/rope through holes - Madeline).
- Use more than 1 ball during the activity - **Egg Drop Soup**. How many tennis balls can you get across?
- If you're up for making 2 apparat-eyes, pit 2 groups against each other and see how competition factors into productivity.
- Vary the size of the receptacle - the smaller the more difficult.

ADDITIONAL IDEAS:
- **Hole-In-One** equipment can also be used with: **Birthday Rope, Rope Bus, & Trolleys**.

NEEDS: One plastic milk crate (legally obtained). Four one-gallon jugs filled with water. I like to use the pop-off lids when I do this one outside. This way if a jug (egg) is dropped and the top pops off, it will resemble the breaking of an egg. (Avoid the pop-off lids inside, it's just a big old mess - use the screw on lids). One 4' length of rope (used in **Trolleys**) for each player. Set the crate (nest) tipped over on its side. Set the jugs of water (eggs) varying distances from the crate and from each other.

PROCEDURE: As the group is walking along to the next activity, unbeknownst to you and the group, you happen upon an endangered Monstrasoarous nest. It looks as though you must have scared off some animal in the middle of trying to rob the nest of its four eggs. Doing your duty as endangered animal activists, you decide to re-nest the eggs. "Surely," you say, "there must be some regulations on returning these eggs to the nest." You check your files (in your pack) for the right documentation. "Ah-Ha!" you cry, "here they are" (see p. 89 for "Endangered Species Re-Nesting Policy").

"And I just happen to have some tempered ropes with me," you add with a wistful sense of pride. Surely this is all in fun.

The idea is to lift the milk jugs off the ground and set them back into the crate. The concept with the ropes is for each person to have a hold of one rope, then grab the end of another player's rope in a fashion that will cradle the egg for transport. As a leader, you have to decide what "heavy" drops are. If the drop would break an egg, then count that one lost. Failure is a learning process and very process worthy indeed.

OBSERVATIONS/QUESTIONS:
- How did you feel about these "Re-nesting" procedures?
- What was the most difficult part of the activity?
- How were you able to overcome the situation?
- What kinds of "silly procedures" do you have to follow at home/work?
- What's another name for procedures? Why are rules important?
- If we could change some rules in this activity, what would you change?
- What would you change at home/work?
- How successful were you? Was there failure? Is it okay to fail?
- What would be important about failure?
- Were you successful? In what ways?

(other) ·

     ·

VARIATIONS:
- •When I do this with youth groups, I allow them to whisper (this tends to be very hard for them - the whisper part).
- •Instead of putting the jugs into the crate, have the group put them on top of the bottom (you gotta flip the crate upside down - but you knew this right?) - a bit more tricky.
- •Here's some fun I tried the other day. Create a large rope circle around the crate. Call this the "Nocuous Zone" (dead animal parts rotting and all that stuff). Any player that enters this area will need protective eyewear/blind-folds.

ADDITIONAL **I**DEAS:
- •**Goodness Cratious** equipment can also be used with: **Birthday Rope, Rope Bus, Tangles** & **Hole-In-One**.

ENDANGERED SPECIES RE-NESTING POLICY

1) Any re-nesting activity must be done in silence so as not to attract the mother back to the nest, possibly devouring the re-nesters.

2) Special tempered ropes must be used to avoid human contact with the eggs (see Note). Due to the nature of these ropes, each re-nester can hold onto only one end of the rope they choose. Once they grab the rope, this hand cannot be removed until all the eggs are back in the nest.

3) Eggs must never be dragged or rolled along the ground. These motions may affect the normal development of the occupant.

4) If there are any unusual holes through the eggs, do not place any ropes through them. These holes are too fragile to be weighted upon.

5) Always use great care when moving eggs. Any heavy drops will surely cause damage and endanger its occupant.

6) Failure to follow these rules will result in strict penalties determined by the time of the year. And Good Luck to you all.

Note: Human contact with an egg will leave a scent. This human scent will cause the mother to abandon the eggs, thus leaving them for nature's way.

THOUGHTS · NOTES · REVELATIONS

DESCEND-SION

Thanks to Sam Sikes.

NEEDS: When Sam and I first talked about this, he had tried **Descend-sion** with a long tent pole. However, when I looked through the resources in this book, there were several options. You could use the "arms" from the PVC **Bun-G-Box**. Every 3 players could use 1 arm section. You could also use the 3/4" PVC from **The Cube**, the **Leakers'** tubes, or some of those Foam Noodles described in the **Three Noodle Initiatives**.

PROCEDURE: Give each small group of 3 one of the PVC arms (or other long prop) from the **Bun-G-Box**. Line up the players so 2 players are on one side of the arm, standing near the ends, and the other player is on the other side of the arm facing the other two players, standing near the middle of the arm (see diagram).

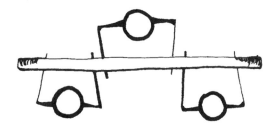

Now, have all the players make little guns with their hands: thumb up, pointer finger straight out and all the rest curled in. Hold the guns up about chest high. Then put the **Bun-G-Box** arm across the top of the barrels of each player's gun. There should be 6 fingers touching the underside of the PVC arm. Now they are ready for a little "Descend-sion."

Ask the group (or all the groups you have) to lower the PVC arm to the ground and set it down. All 6 fingers need to be in contact with the PVC at all times. If a finger un-touches the PVC, the group must start again at chest height. Also, players may not pinch the PVC with their thumbs to hold it down. The PVC is meant to just lay upon the top of the pointer fingers. Sounds easy? Give it a shot.

OBSERVATIONS/QUESTIONS:
- What was the initial reaction to the activity?
- Was there any planning before it was attempted?
- Did anything unexpected happen? What adjustments were made to compensate for any problems?
- How did the group communicate with each other?
- Was there any frustration?
- Were you honest about the rules?
- What was the reaction of the players when someone un-touched?

•What skill(s) did you need to acquire to find success? What was successful for you? How did you measure your success?

(other) •

       •

VARIATIONS:

•Buy some 1" PVC straight couplings and make longer sections for more people
to try the activity together. What happens to the task as the group (company) gets bigger?
•Use the 45° couplings from the PVC **Bun-G-Box** and connect pipes in a zig-zag
line or a circle. Which shape is easier?

ADDITIONAL IDEAS:

OVERHEAD CRANE

Thanks to Clay Fiske and Lori Armstrong.

I want to add a little historic evolution to this one. *Jiggle and Swiggle* from Terry Orlick's, "The Second Cooperative Sports and Game Book," 1982, was my first encounter with the apparatus. Then it was resurrected in 1996 in Karl Rohnke's, "FUNN Stuff, Vol. 1," under the name, *Plunging the Depths of Psyche Center*. Now the activity moves yet another step up the evolutionary chain. And they say there is no progress!

NEEDS: You'll need a crane (this will not be a bird - however, I have seen some of these cranes fly!). If you use an arm from the PVC **Bun-G-Box** (see p. 109), you'll be halfway there. (If not, you can make one with a dowel rod.) Let's say we're going to use the **Bun G-Box** arm. Each arm will accommodate 2 players. You'll also need a 42" piece of 3/8" string for each crane, and a large "S" hook. These are the supplies for the crane for 2 players. So, if you have more players, you'll need to do some math.

Now you will need some building supplies. I like to use 3 plastic cups for each pair of builders. I like to have 2 cups the same size and 1 a different size. The cups will need a "hooking" point. I burn small holes in the bottom of the cups and bolt a small eye bolt to each - with the eye part sticking up from the bottom on the outside of the cup (see diagram). However, you need not be so fancy. You could use paper clips and/or twist ties too. Now you're ready.

PROCEDURE: (Keep in mind I will be referring to one small group of 2 players as builders. You can do multiple groups as well, each pair with their own crane and building supplies.)

Place the cups at point "A" loading zone, and cordon off a point "B" building zone anywhere from 10' to 20' away. Now give the group the **Bun-G-Box** arm, the string, and the "S" hook. They must construct a crane that will transport the cups to the building zone and build a three cup pyramid. During loading, the transport of the cups, and the building of the pyramid, no part of the crane or the cups may be touched by any part of either player's arms (an arm being the shoulder to the finger tips). Placing the last cup tends to be the most interesting procedure. If you don't allow them to touch the crane after it is put together, the pairs will have to spin the rope around the PVC to get the S hook higher in order to pick the last cup up higher. How will they adapt to the change in process?

OBSERVATION/QUESTIONS:

- What was your overall reaction to the activity?
- What ideas were generated by the small building groups?
- Did groups share ideas? Did groups use other player's ideas? Did anyone copy another group's idea? Was this okay?
- What unforeseen challenges did you encounter? How were they taken care of?
- How were the guidelines interpreted? Were the interpretations within the parameters of how the activity was set up?
- Which group finished first? What was the reaction?
- Did groups help each other? How was the help interpreted?
- Were you successful? In what way?

(other) •

     •

VARIATIONS:

- You could use 1" dowel rods for the crane.
- Have small groups work together to build a little city.
- Karl Rohnke uses a thicker dowel and puts new plunger cups on each end of the dowel. Then he uses 16" of small diameter cord - ties one end to the middle of the rod, the other to a tennis ball (small slit in the ball, knot in the rope, knot into the slit). Two players squeeze this apparatus between them - at forehead, chest, or waist area, then sway their bodies around to cause the ball to spin around the dowel rod till it can spin no more.
- For an easy start, let players touch the crane with their hands during transportation and building. From this point you could progress to the no-touch rule.

ADDITIONAL IDEAS:

CARPET MAZE

NEEDS: One Carpet Maze and a buzzer if you can find one (not necessary but fun). The maze is made by using a 6' x 10' piece of material (I use a tarp) and with 1" strips of duct tape (you may have to tear a 2" roll), make a pattern of squares 1' x 1'. There should be 60 squares on a 6' x 10' maze. Also, I like to use a set of numbered 3" x 5" cards to hand out so the players remember their order during the activity.

PROCEDURE: The group must discover a hidden pattern within the maze (predetermined by the facilitator) without verbal communication. (Allow five minutes for planning.) Only 1 player can touch the maze at a time, and players must follow each other in the same order at all times (this is where the numbered card help). A buzzing noise indicates an incorrect square (I do a vocal buzz if I don't have an electric one). After being buzzed, the player must exit the EXACT same way as he/she entered, or they will be buzzed again. The next person in order enters the maze. Set a buzz goal for motivation.

This is a nice low risk element with great learning potential. Copy the Carpet Maze template provided on p. 97 (make some extras while you're at it for future games). Then map out a pattern on the template for your activity. The more advanced the group, the more complex the maze can be. Explain to the group that the pattern must be found, and every square in the pattern must be used. Give the group their 5 minutes to plan, then they must start the activity.

The hard part of facilitation is watching the pattern and the group dynamics at the same time. It is really helpful to have another staff member watch the pattern so you can watch the group.

OBSERVATIONS/QUESTIONS:
- How was the 5 minutes of planning used? Who was the leader?
- What was it like to be BUZZED?
- What kind of help did the players on the maze look for? None? Group?
- Who took responsibility for the buzzes?
- What was the hardest part about the activity?
- What is important about communication? What type was used?
- What did it take to be successful?..taking a risk?..failing?
- Is it hard to accept failure? What if it is needed to be successful?

(other) •

  •

VARIATIONS:
- Make three different maze patterns - easy to more challenging. Then when the group gathers for this one, you can ask them what level of challenge they would like - providing more "challenge by choice."
- If you are prepared for anarchy, try this. Change the last square for one person in the group (without telling until you process). This is a great metaphor on discrimination. Some people are not allowed to do what others get to do. This involves risk, so be selective with groups.
- Set a time limit.
- Limit the number of buzzes before starting over.
- Use Poly Spots or Plastic Canvases for the squares of the maze (see Note in **Lily Pads & Islands**).
- See **Bun-G-Box** for another variation of a maze.
- Sam Sikes has a great variation he uses for corporate groups (as well as with larger groups) found in "Feeding the Zircon Gorilla." His tarp is 8' x 12' marked out in 1' x 1' squares using masking tape. (I'm not sure how long masking tape will last, but it's already one inch!) His maze pattern forms a large "S" shape that touches both sides of the tarp. In this way, multiple groups can work together to discover the pattern. Any time they make the same mistake more than once, resources are taken away–he gives out pennies. When all the money is used up, the company goes into debt. Get a copy of his book - great stuff!!
- Check out **The Last Crusade** for another great twist to the **Carpet Maze**.

ADDITIONAL **I**DEAS:
- Progress to the **Carpet Maze** from the **Tarp Activities**.

CARPET MAZE
TEMPLATE

THE LAST CRUSADE & THE PATH TO ENLIGHTENMENT ©

Great thanks to Tom Leahy for this one.

I appreciated the creative process of this activity the first time I saw it. The way it engaged the group was dynamic. This one also inspired the activity rhyme in **Chris-Cross**.

I have to say, if you are looking for any training in the field of Experiential Education, Leahy & Associates is my recommendation to you. Also, if you remember back in the credits, Tom was the one to coin the title for this book. All my thanks to you, Tom! Now, off to The Last Crusade....

NEEDS: Tom uses 34 plastic canvas pieces as the "stepping stones" for his version and tapes the symbols on the stones (see diagram on p. 101). He cuts 10 1/2" x 13 1/2" plastic canvas sheets in half to make his stones. (See the Note in **Lily Pads & Islands** for more information on the canvases).

You could also use the 6' x 10' Carpet Maze (see the Needs section of the **Carpet Maze** activity for construction instructions). Then you will have to add the markings shown on the pattern diagram. The diagrams provided, have Tom's version as it looks with canvas squares (pg. 101), and his version with the solution (pg. 102). If you use the Carpet Maze tarp, I have added dotted lines to the solution diagram to show the additional tarp material and pattern (pg. 102).

PROCEDURE: Give the group a copy of The Last Crusade riddle (p. 99). Using this information, the group must uncover "The Path to Enlightenment." As a facilitator, you can use the Interpretations sheet (p. 100) to monitor the activity. Then just sit back and buzz!

OBSERVATION/QUESTIONS: (I'm going to let you run with these.)

ADDITIONAL IDEAS:
- Plastic Canvases can also be used with: **Boundary Ball, Lily Pads & Islands, Islands, Corporate Box** & **Mine Field**.

THE LAST CRUSADE

The field before, you all must cross
to reach your goal with minimum loss.

Just like a cat, numbered lives you'll have,
when you choose poorly, one less for your path.

From side to side at times you'll track,
move ever forward, never back.

One more direction will break the heart,
of one who tries to quicken the mark.

Step by step, you'll travel on,
skip no row, or lose a pawn.

Some stones among the field are signed,
to aid your path and guide your line.

When at last the goal you near,
caution now for danger is clear.

This initiative was created after inspiration from the movie "Indiana Jones and the Last Crusade." The scene is late in the movie where Indy is trying to cross the stone passage, and the necessity to move from stone to stone is significant. There is only one path through the field, but no jumping is allowed for safety reasons. Participants are not allowed to mark or move the stones in any way.

> The field before, you all must cross
> to reach your goal with minimum loss.

All team members must cross the field with at least one life remaining.

> Just like a cat, numbered lives you will have,
> when you choose poorly, one less for your path.

The collective team has nine lives. A life is lost with each incorrect move. Any individual who steps on an incorrect stone simply returns to the start. No team member is ever removed from the game.

> From side to side at times you'll track,
> move ever forward, never back.

Only two directions of movement are allowed for this game, forward and sideways. No moves are allowed 'backwards' (either retracing steps or moving toward the starting line).

> One more direction will break the heart,
> of one who tries to quicken the mark.

No diagonal moves are allowed. Moving to any space in a diagonal direction will cost a life.

> Step by step you'll travel on,
> skip no row, or lose a pawn.

In accounting, rows are horizontal and columns are vertical. Players are not allowed to jump over a row, or they lose a life.

> Some stones among the field are signed,
> to aid your path and guide your line.

Two stones are marked with symbols, in this case the Greek letters Lambda and Chi. While the symbols themselves have no significant meaning to the game, they do mark 'good' choices and one points to the exit (and the symbol opening is in the direction of the 'opening' to the maze when you use the Carpet Maze tarp).

> When at last the goal you near,
> caution now for danger is clear.

Nothing significant in the pattern, but groups tend to get sloppy when the end is in sight.

THE LAST CRUSADE-
TOM'S VERSION

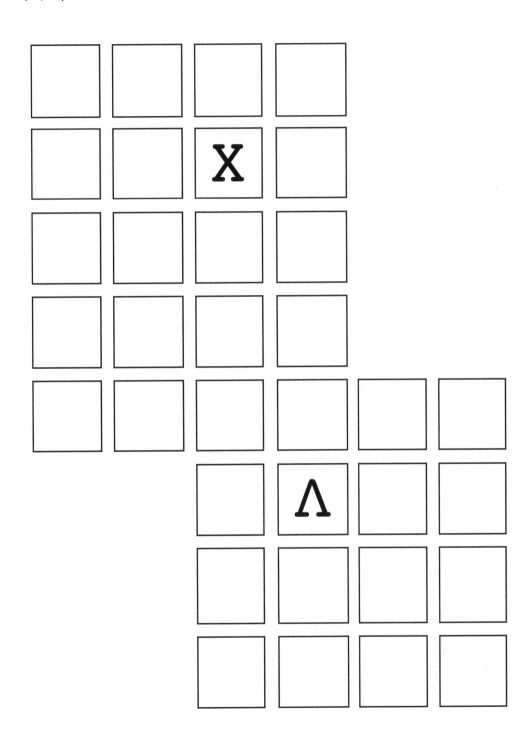

THE LAST CRUSADE-
THE CORRECT PATH

END

TOM'S STEPPING STONES

CARPET MAZE ADDITION

START

WOOD VERSION

FYI - Please don't be discouraged by the Needs list. Once this element is functional you will be glad you made the effort. I also have a PVC version following this one. It's a bit easier to get together. So, why keep the wood version? Sentimental reasons I guess.

NEEDS: This activity requires 2" x 4"s: 2 end pieces measured at 5' 10" and 4 side pieces measured at 4' 7" long (two 12', 2" x 4"s will do the trick. You need some corner pieces mentioned below). All the 2" x 4"s will be drilled with 5/8" holes 10" apart (see diagram). The 2 side pieces will be held together by a strong door hinge, so you'll need a total of 2 'strong' door hinges. (Hinges are an option for storage and transportation purposes. They do have a disadvantage, however, that I've listed below in the Facilitation/Safety section.) You'll also need 73' of 3/8" bungee cord (some hardware stores carry it or could order it for you. The next best suggestion would be to mail order it from REI - see Equipment Catalogs in appendix section). Cut the bungee in 10 - 4' pieces and 6 - 5'6" pieces. After cutting, put an overhand knot on a bite in each end of each piece of bungee. This will give you a little loop to put the dowel pins through to hold the cords in the frame. So, that means you will need a total of 32 small dowel pins. (What's a dowel pin? It's a little wooden piece with grooves in it that woodworkers use to glue together pieces of wood when they don't want to use nails. Ask the hardware guy or gal, they will know.) Finally you'll need 4 - 2" x 4" x 4" blocks of wood for your corners. Then at each corner you'll want to put in a <u>locking</u> screen door latch - the hook into the eye bolt thing. Clear? If you're a visual learner, see if the Set-Up plans (p. 102) help. If not, make up your own!!

You'll also need some Boxes from the **Roof Tops** activity to elevate the element - or use anything else that will work for elevation. The number of Boxes will depend on the level of difficulty you seek (see "Note" below). Also, depending on the activity you decide to do, there are other props needed. See Procedure and Variations for any other items. (Please refer to Set-Up plans for more details on the **Bun-G-Box** construction materials.)

Note: Use Boxes to vary the degree of difficulty. Using 1 Box at each corner will make the activity easier than using 3 Boxes. In the case of the **Horizontal Web** variation, more Boxes will make it easier.

BUN-G-BOX CONSTRUCTION AND SET UP PLANS

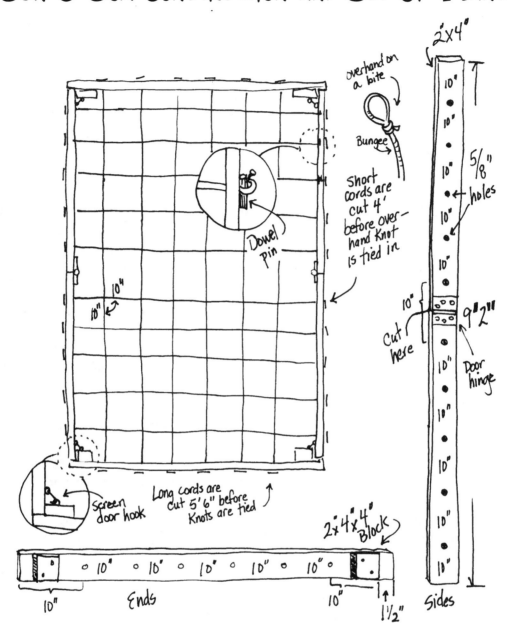

2×4"

overhand on a bite

Bungee

Short cords are cut 4' before over-hand Knot is tied in

Dowel Pin

10" 10"

10"

10"

10"

10"

5/8" holes

Cut here

9'2"

Door hinge

10"

10"

10"

10"

10"

10"

Screen door hook

Long cords are cut 5'6" before Knots are tied

2"×4"×4" Block

10" · 10" · 10" · 10" · 10" ·

Ends

10"

10"

1½"

Sides

BUN-G-BOX SIDE VIEW

ELEVATE WITH BOXES

Affordable Portables © 1999 Chris Cavert & Wood 'N' Barnes Publishing & Distribution

affordable portables

PROCEDURE: **Cuppling**. After setting up the Bun-G-Box - placing it at the height appropriate for your group - place large plastic cups at each bungee crossing. (Next time you're in Vegas, pick up some 'free' coin cups at the Casinos - who me? I never have, I've just heard about it). Placing the cups at the intersections will take a little balancing, but it's possible.

The quest is for all the players to get through the Bun-G-Box as quickly as possible - a timed event. So what's with the cups? If a cup is knocked off, one of two things can happen: 1) Nothing, or 2) Something. Let me explain the "something" as best I can. Each cup on the bungee cords is overlapping 4 squares in the Bun-G-Box. Any square that is overlapped by a cup is open to step in. Now, when a cup falls, the squares that it was overlapping may have other cups activating them; however, as more cups fall there will be squares that are not overlapped by a cup. These squares are then closed and cannot be stepped in. Good luck!

FACILITATION/SAFETY: After using this activity, I ran into a few interesting points I need to share. If the bungee is too tight, it tends to pull in the sides where the hinges are. This causes excessive stress in this area and tends to work the screws out of the hinges. To avoid this, just use single side pieces 80" long. Also, <u>make sure</u> you use the locking door hooks at the corners. Before this was suggested to me, there were some implosion events occurring - bungees like to contract if not held securely at bay.

OBSERVATIONS/QUESTIONS:
  •How was your plan devised? Who took the "initiative?"
  •How many ideas were generated before you started?
  •Was anyone apprehensive about the plan? Did you speak up?
  •Did anyone have another idea that wasn't shared? What was it?
  •In what order did the group decide to go in? Was there any consensus about the order? In what way does "order" affect this activity?
  •Who was first, who was last, and is this a common occurrence?
  •What part of the success (or failure) did you feel a part of?
  •What made the activity fun?..not fun?
  •What kinds of support were evident? What support was needed to be successful? What was helpful about it?
(other) •
        •

HORIZONTAL WEB SET-UP OPTIONS

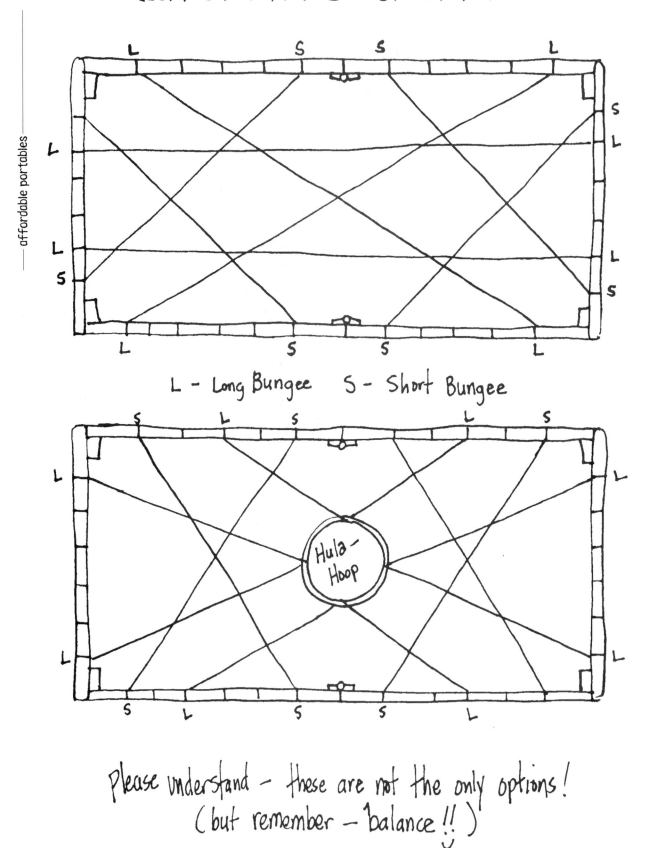

affordable portables

L – Long Bungee   S – Short Bungee

Please understand – these are not the only options!
(but remember – balance !!)

VARIATIONS:
- **Coupling** - Do the activity holding hands with a partner.
- Try the same activity with water or beans in the cups.
- Try a 3-D Maze. Read the **Carpet Maze** activity description, you'll get the idea. Set the Bun-G-Box on the ground. If they touch the cord while uncovering the path, the maze changes. I give the group markers for this one. Once they place a marker, however, it cannot be picked up (this is really tough!).
- **House Trap** - This one is similar to **Cuppling**. But, instead of putting the cups out before the group starts, give the cups to the participants. You can give out as many cups as you like depending on the level of challenge the group is ready for. Ask the group how many cups they think they need. More challenge by "choices." Each cup is a "key" that can open four doors (placing the cup at a cord intersection opens four spaces). Once a key is placed, it cannot be taken out. However, it can fall into the house, never to be seen again; hence closing the doors the key opened. If someone is standing in a door when it closes, another key must be used to open the door. Did I say anything about holding on to the keys? I like this one.
- **Horizontal Web** - This is an interesting variation or progression to **The Web**. Set the bungee cords in diagonal directions creating a number of larger openings for bodies to pass through (see diagram on p. 105). Set the Bun-G-Box on 3 or 4 levels of Boxes (both choices have their own challenges). Players have to get to a hole of their choice entering from the top without touching any part of the Bun-G-Box, then duck through the hole and out under the Bun-G-Box. The hole then closes. A player can reopen it by crawling under, up and then out of the hole again. This one can be quite intriguing. This version will most probably involve lifting, so always be attentive to safety issues.

My friend Sam Sikes just tapes a string web in between 2 tables for the same effect. Very portable.

PVC BUN-**G**-**B**OX **V**ERSION

NEEDS: I built my first version of this on the floor of my local "big" hardware store. They had a PVC cutting tool that cut up to 1" PVC, so that was the size I used (you could go bigger if you want - going smaller may not hold well, but I haven't tried it yet).

Cut 1" PVC into 8 pieces 2 1/2' long (this is 2 - 10' pipes [the store carries them in this size] cut into 4 sections). I call these "arms." The length of the arms I chose had to do with transportation purposes (and because 2 1/2' goes into 10' quite nicely); however, you can go longer if you want. (FYI - all PVC used is schedule 40 type.) Then you'll need: 8 - 1" 45 degree couplings; 8 - Ts, 1 1/4" x 1 1/4" x 1"; 24 - 3/16" x 2 1/2" eye bolts; and 24 #10 coarse thread lock nuts (these are the self-locking nuts with the plastic insets). For the legs, I have 2 sizes: 8 - 1" x 12" and 8 - 1" x 17" lengths. (If you plan it out right you will end up with less PVC waste as you can get your eight 12" and eight 18" legs out of two 1" x 10' PVC pipes.) Then for the bungee part you'll need 4 of those really small quick links and 70' of 7/64" bungee cord (I got mine from REI - there's info in the Equipment Catalogs in the Appendix section). I cut the cord in half (35') and put in a couple of overhand knots on a bite to give me a couple of loops to put the quick links into.

Now you'll have to do a little work (unless of course you can figure out an easier way around this - if you can, please let me know). You need 3 - 3/16" holes drilled in each arm. One in the center of the arm - 15" from either end, and one 5" from either end of the arm. All of the holes should be in the same "line" so when the eye bolts go in they will all be at the same level. Place the eye bolts in and then screw on the nuts. The eye bolt holes should set parallel to the ground if you set the arm on the ground (see diagram, p. 109). Unfortunately, there will be threads sticking out from the nuts. I hack-sawed mine off for safety reasons - plus it looks really nice. Your choice. I think that's everything. Now check out the Set-Up diagram (p. 109).

Here are a few Set-Up tips. Lay out the arms on the floor, slip a T piece over each arm and then put on the 45. Make sure you purchase 45's that fit snuggly into the 1 1/4 section of the T's. After it's all laid out, push everything together. If you're worried about loose fits, cut some rubber bands up and stick a little piece between each connection. Don't forget to put the 1" part of the T facing open toward the ground so you can put the legs in. Choose your leg height (I use the 12" for **Cuppling**, **Coupling**, and **House Trap**; I use the 18" for **Horizontal Web**), slap them in there and then you're ready for the bungee.

For the square grid pattern I marked out the way I string it on the diagram with one solid line for one 35' piece, and a dotted line for the other 35' piece. For the web, I've only needed one 35' piece. I'll let you come up with your own design. If you've gotten this far, I'm sure you can handle it. It's a lot better if there is someone to help string this up with you to watch for twists and stuff. ("What is stuff?" you ask. Well that's all in the fun of discovering, isn't it?)

So once you have this looking like any one of the pictures I drew (or not), try one of the activities described above. Let the games begin!!

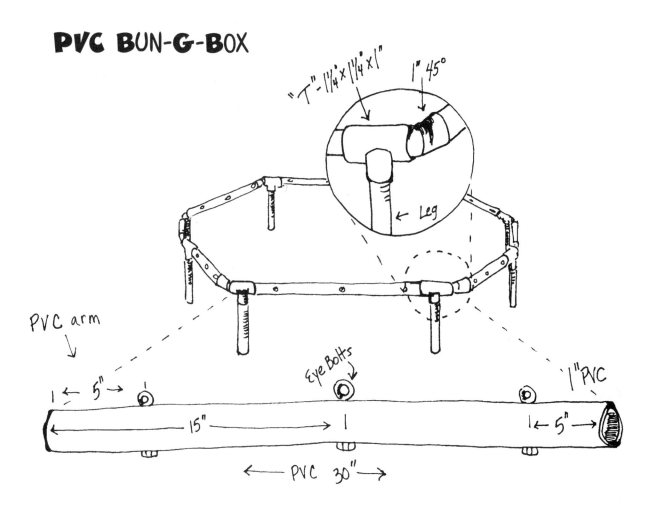

PVC BUN-G-BOX

"T"-1¼"×1¼"×1"

1" 45°

Leg

PVC arm

1 ← 5" → 1

Eye Bolts

1"PVC

15"   1

1 ← 5" →

← PVC 30" →

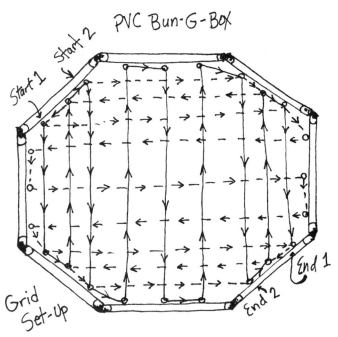

Start 1   Start 2   PVC Bun-G-Box

Grid Set-Up

End 1

End 2

LINES OF COMMUNICATION

Thanks to Sam Sikes, "Feeding the Zircon Gorilla."

NEEDS: The first thing you will need is the PVC **Bun-G-Box** frame and legs (see **Bun-G-Box**, PVC variation). When you set the arms, point the eye bolts down so they are perpendicular to the ground. You'll need 8 - 1" PVC couplings to connect between the 12" legs and the 17" legs to make one long leg coming out of each "T". Now the PVC **Bun-G-Box** frame sits 29" off the ground with the eyes of the bolts pointing down.

Then you will need - the Hover Pad. Mine consists of 12 - 8' strings and a cheap plastic flying disc with a good size rim on it. Here's the extra work - drill 12 small holes (large enough to fit your pieces of string through) equally spaced apart around the rim of the disc. Put the strings through the holes and knot the ends so the string cannot come out. Now you have this "Daddy Long Leg" looking thing - this is your Hover Pad.

The last thing you will need is something to move or cover. You could move a cup - empty or full, a ball or two or three, a hot wheels car, a piece of fruit - whatever works for you. You could cover poly spots, playing cards, pine cones, or plastic frogs. Now, how does it work?

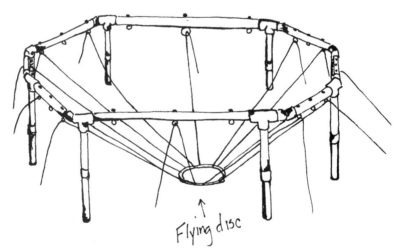

Flying disc

PROCEDURE: Place the disc on the floor/ground within the center of the Bun-G-Box frame (we'll call this the space station). Rim up or down, it will be your choice. Pull a string through every other eye of the eye bolts on the PVC Arms and man (or woman) each string (you can play with groups of 12 using 1 string each - or 6 using 2 strings each).

I like to start with covering things. Put a bunch of "things" inside the space station. Have the group work the strings to move the Hover Pad around and down to cover different items. Doing this will give them practice and define their range of movement.

After some practice, set out some spots in a triangle shape in the space station. The distance apart will be determined by the items they were able to cover during the first round. Now, starting the Hover Pad at one spot, put an empty cup on the pad. Have the group move the cup to another pad. If successful, fill the cup with beans or water. Have them move it to another pad. May the force be with you!

Note: This is not easy. Make sure your group is ready to go through a lot of trial and error without a high level of frustration. If there is too much failure, you might want to consider moving to another activity and then come back to this one later.

OBSERVATIONS/QUESTIONS:
- What did you learn by doing this activity?
- How did the group communicate with each other?
- Was everyone a part of the activity?
- What part did each person have in the process?
- Did anyone just drop a string? For what reason?
- How many attempts did you make before you had some success? Is this common in every-day life? In what areas?
- How did the group work through their frustration?
- What did it take to see some success? Is there always success?

(other) •
          •

VARIATIONS:
- Try it with the space station just one foot off the ground.
- Try moving fruit into a basket, frogs into a bowl, or marbles into a jar.
- Here's a great Sikes' variation: Take paper plates, give them a dollar value (both negative and positive values) and place them in the playing area inside the space station. Put a loop of masking tape on each plate so the disc can pick them up off the floor if it is set on the plate (the rim will have to be placed up for this one). Inform the team they have 15 minutes once they start, to make as much money as they can. To make money, plates have to be picked up by the disc, brought to the edge of the PVC structure and removed by a player. Add up (and subtract) what money you get after 15 minutes.
- Use a Bull Ring (Cain & Jolliff, 1998) as a hover pad.

ADDITIONAL **I**DEAS:

SECTION safety first TWO

THOUGHTS · NOTES · REVELATIONS

Let's think about that top five list I mentioned earlier. Top on the list will most definitely be safety. Safety is always first and foremost in an experiential facilitator's mind - with no compromise! Because of the many risks involved in experiential education, the safety we refer to has two components: physical safety and emotional safety. Neither one is less important than the other. Again, I strongly encourage further exploration into these topics so you will better understand the full scope of the process.

This brief section of activities is intended to prepare you and your group to take the "next step" along the progression. Before moving into the Initiative Elements, you will want to prepare your group to keep its players physically safe as they participate in activities that take them off the ground. These activities will also take the group into "Trust and Empathy" issues (mentioned in the Initiative Games introduction). Move carefully through these activities and do not progress too fast. Make sure the group is ready (safety wise) to engage in the elements. You can always go back to the Initiative stage to give them more time to build the needed interaction and trust before moving on.

Practice the spotting technique, described on the following page, using the activities in this section. Once you feel the group is ready, move into the Initiative Elements.

Spotting is a term that means actively protecting the progress of another participant. A "human safety net," of sorts. The spotter's main purpose is to help prevent falls from causing injury. The spotter's primary duty is to protect the head and upper body of a participant using physical support.

A spotter does not hold up a participant, but is ready to protect if a fall occurs. Participants must realize that a spotter's duty is not to prevent a fall, it is to prevent injury. So, if both the spotter and participant end up on the ground without serious harm, the spotter has done his job.

There are 2 rules of correct spotting recommended by the Outdoor Institute of North Carolina (Wall, DeLano, & DeLano, 1991, p. 8):

1. Always pay **Attention.** The spotter must always watch the participant.
2. Fall **Anticipation.** The spotter is always ready with hands up.

The basic spotting position should be taught to all participants. This position can then be modified to fit the needs of each activity.

BASIC **S**POTTING **P**OSITION: The basic spot is arms up, slightly bent with hands open, one leg back from the other with foot turned out and knees slightly bent (see illustration). A spotter does not want to be rigid in the joints but rather absorbent so a participant is caught smoothly without being jolted to a stop.

TENNIS BALL WALK

NEEDS: 40 to 60 old tennis balls (find these at clubs or schools, they are often willing to give them away if you tell them you work with kids), and a hard flat surface (like a court or floor) 15' long.

PROCEDURE: Establish a tight rectangular pattern of tennis balls on the ground, about 3' wide and 10' long. Divide the group in half standing on the long sides of the rectangle. Choose a participant to go first and place that person at one of the ends. The group members on the sides assume the basic spotting position (please read intro to this section). The active participant (AP) attempts to walk down the lane, on top of the balls, without touching the ground (yes, it is possible). Instruct the group to spot at all times but not to hold the AP up on the tennis balls. A facilitator should walk behind each AP. Give everyone a chance to try. Stress good spotting! If you're using this activity to introduce and practice spotting, choose a reliable person to walk behind the AP so you are free to walk around and evaluate spotting techniques.

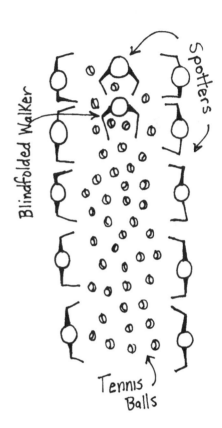

OBSERVATIONS/QUESTIONS:
- Was the activity difficult?
- What were the reactions of the walkers?
- Did you feel safe going through the gauntlet?
- What behaviors encouraged safety in this group?
- How would the activity be if there were no spotters?
- What is important about spotting?

(other) •

•

VARIATION:
- Try the activity with a blindfold (after the sighted way).
- Have 2 players move from point "A" to point "B" using 6 tennis balls - without touching the ground of course.

ADDITIONAL **I**DEAS:

NEEDS: Three or four 4" x 4" x 8' boards (used in the **Friendship Walk** element), blindfolds for one third of the group, and a large open area.

PROCEDURE: Set up the boards in a zig-zag pattern on the ground. Divide the group into teams of 3 and ask 1 person to be the Active Participant (AP) for the first round. The AP will walk the length of the beams as the 2 partners follow alongside the person.

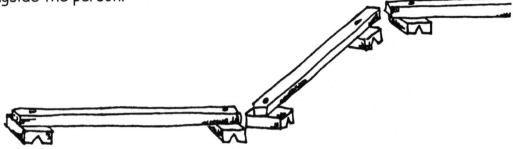

A moving spot is done here. Spotters' arms and hands should be up around the AP's shoulder area (not touching the AP). Instruct the spotters never to cross one leg over another. This causes a weak stance. (Please be sure to read all of the Spotting information found at the front of this section.)

Have every group of 3, and every person who wants to, take turns walking the zig-zag pattern sighted. Once a group leaves the first board, start another group. After everyone has tried the zig-zag sighted, add a blindfold for the second round through. This makes it a bit more challenging and risky. Keep reinforcing the "2 rules of spotting." Stop any unsafe actions so the trust level of your group and its participants stays in tact.

OBSERVATIONS/QUESTIONS:
- Which way was the hardest? Sighted or blinded?
- Could you make the entire way without stepping off?
- How were the spotters being helpful?
- When you were a spotter, what was the hardest thing you had to do?
- How many had a hard time paying attention to proper spotting?
- Did any of the participants fall to the ground? Why?
- What is important about spotting?

(other) •

•

VARIATIONS:

- For a level progression - to provide choices for players - make the first section a masking tape line on the floor (or a rope line for outside). The next level can be a 4" x 4" x 8' board on the floor. For the third level, bolt each end of the next board to a box (from the **Roof Tops** element) with 5/8" x 5 1/2" carriage bolts. Then have the last (if you want to go this long) 4" x 4" x 8' board on the ground. In this way participants have an option to skip a level if they want.
- Here's a good leadership activity. Blindfold all but 1 or 2 group members. Have the blindfolded players line up behind the first board and place their hands on the shoulders of the person in front of them. Now have the leaders lead, and take care of, the group through the zig-zag. At the end of the journey I like to ask the group to rate the leadership and give feedback. Then choose 2 other leaders to walk the group through. Hopefully they will use the feedback given to other leaders to be better leaders themselves.
- How about walking the pattern backward?
- Set up obstacles over the boards that players have to go over or under.
- There is a new resource that I recently discovered that works very well for this activity - white vinyl fence posts. I found them in the lawn and garden section in one of those big hardware stores. (Sorry, no free advertising here!) They are lighter than boards and hold up very well. I've only used them with little kids so far. I haven't tested them out on the big kids yet. Let me know how they work.

ADDITIONAL **I**DEAS:

—WARNING BELLS———————

NEEDS: 2 blindfolds, 2 bell-balls (balls with bells in them [cat toys] or film containers with BBs inside) and an open area for a large circle.

PROCEDURE: Form a large size circle in an open area. Choose 2 volunteers who are willing to be blindfolded. From the 2, pick a tagger and a taggee. Put the blindfolds on. The leader moves each person around in the circle somewhere, then carefully hands each a bell-ball without giving away the other person's position.

The tagger must find and tag the other person. The tagger is allowed 3 separate rings with the ball, to which the taggee must answer with a ring each time. However, the taggee can ring as many times as he/she wishes, and the tagger must answer each time. The rest of the group acts as silent bumpers to prevent the 2 players from leaving the circle. Silence is very important in this game (and often the hardest part of the process). When the tagger finally tags the taggee or his 3 rings are used up without tagging, switch rolls to give the taggee a chance to be a tagger. The round is over after a tag or 3 rings. Choose 2 other players. Play enough times to give everyone a chance to play both roles.

OBSERVATIONS/QUESTIONS:
    •What was it like being blindfolded?
    •What qualities does it take to be blindfolded in front of other people?
    •What was it like to be the tagger? Did you have a plan?
    •What was it like to be the taggee? Did you have a strategy?
    •What role did the rest of the group have?
    •Did everyone in the group follow directions?
    •What happens when people don't follow directions?
    •Could you share your level of trust with group members?
    •What types of things bring down trust levels?
(other) •
        •

VARIATIONS:
    •Only blindfold the tagger. When the tagger rings, the sighted taggee has 3 seconds to answer (3 seconds to move around in the circle). When the taggee answers the ring - with a ring - she must stay still until the tagger either tags her or rings the bell-ball again.
    •Play outside in a leafy area without the bell-balls. It will be important to have very quiet circle protectors for this one.

•For smaller groups I like to play this way. Have a blindfolded player sit In-
dian-style in the center of a large circle of players. Place the bell-ball 1' in
front of the blindfolded player - I'll shake it before I put it down. Now pick
someone to get the ball without being touched by the blindfolded player. The
blindfolded player can only move his/her arms to tag a sighted stealer - he/
she is not allowed to get up. If the ball is successfully taken, have the stealer
be the new protector. This is a great one outside in the leaves!

ADDITIONAL IDEAS:

MINE FIELD

Thanks to Karl Rohnke, "The Bottomless Bag Again."

NEEDS: A lot of small objects for obstacles (you can use any other equipment from other activities), blindfolds for half the group and a medium-size open area to play. Old rope for boundaries is helpful but not needed. The best situation includes a court with lines already available.

PROCEDURE: Create a large Mine Field with various objects (the more the better), rearrange all the objects so that they are randomly and equally spaced within a rectangular shaped area about 15' x 40'. Border the area with rope or tape.

Pair up group members in any way you choose. Give each pair a blindfold. The objective will be for one partner to cross the Mine Field blindfolded without touching any of the objects or mines (you can see, the more objects, the better). The sighted partner, who is standing on the outside of the Mine Field throughout the activity, is not allowed to touch the blindfolded partner while she/he is on the Field. Provide time for each person to try the activity a couple of times.

If it is possible, work in groups of 3 with 1 member timing the pass through the Mine Field. For each object the blind trekker touches, add 30 seconds to their time. If timing is not possible, count the number of touches for a player and try to lower it the second time. Even better, add the number of touches both partners obtain together and try to do better a second time.

If you can make a large mine field, all the pairs can go at once. This causes some communication difficulty and adds to processability. When partners are done, have them try some of the variations available.

OBSERVATIONS/QUESTIONS:
- What was difficult about the activity?
- How did partners communicate? Did it work?
- What did you learn about communication?
- How did each person feel when the blinded partner touched a Mine?
- Was the trust level affected after a touch?
- What did the sighted partner say after his/her partner touched a Mine?
- What feelings came up during the activity?
- Was there any goal setting done before the activity?
- What was it like to achieve or not achieve your goal?

(other) •
        •

VARIATIONS:
- Blindfolded partner walks backward.
- Every command means the opposite - right means left, big step means small step, bend down means stand up. You get the idea.
- Work in groups of 3. One person guides 2 connected players.
- Karl has some great variations in "Bottomless Bag Again" on p. 53.
- Progress to **Trash Collector**, see the following page.
- I saw this snappy variation at a T.O.T.O. conference in Kansas a while back. Tape (masking) down, in large form, the shape I've provided below. It should be about 5' from side to side. Now lay out a whole bunch of SET mousetraps - the smaller kind! (This takes some time - an initiative in itself.) Now, in groups of 3, have 1 player walk blindfolded through the pattern - shoes are required! Sighted partners can talk from the sides, but may not touch their partner. This could be considered an aerobic activity. Try it to see what I mean. What about a rope pattern outside in the grass? This would add some interesting outcomes.

ADDITIONAL **I**DEAS:

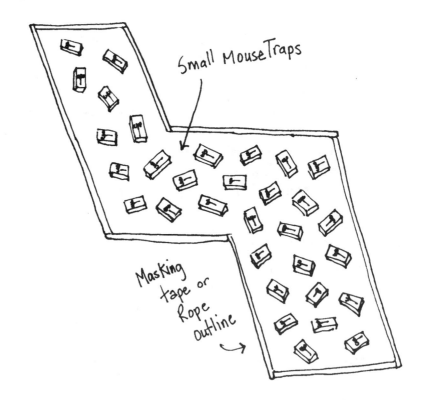

Small Mouse Traps

Masking tape or Rope outline

NEEDS: A lot of small objects, a few blindfolds (depending on group size) and a midsize area to play. (This is a good game to play after **Mine Field** so you can get other people to clean up your stuff!)

PROCEDURE: For the most part, I've only played this after **Mine Field** because the objects are ready to go. If you have a lot of objects, split your group into 3s. If you don't have a lot, split into groups of 4. Give each team a blindfold and a large bag (I use the equipment bags the toys came from - you could also use trash bags). Have them stand outside the boundaries the objects are within.

Here's the game. Each team chooses a trash collector. This person blindfolds him/herself outside the playing field. The sighted players of the group must stay outside the boundaries and remain in contact with the team bag at all times. On the starting signal, the trash collector enters the dump area to collect trash one piece at a time and bring it back, placing the trash in the team bag. Sighted players cannot touch any trash. Group members can verbally tell the trash collector where to go. At no time can the collector in the dump area be touched by any team members.

As the facilitator, I like to designate certain objects as "Freezer Mines." I tell the players that if they touch a freezer mine, in any way, the toucher must stand frozen for 5 Mississippi.

The objective here is to collect as many objects as possible until all that remains are the freezer mines. If you like, count the objects to see who has the most. I never count, it drives the groups crazy!

OBSERVATIONS/QUESTIONS:
- How did groups choose trash collectors?
- What was the communication like between teammates?
- What kind of system was effective for teams?
- Were the rules followed at all times?
- What role did the bag holders take? Who did what?
- What made the activity difficult?
- Was there trust involved in this activity? In what way?
- Who took responsibility for touching a freezer mine?

(other) •
- •

VARIATIONS:
- Switch trash collectors after every 5 pieces of trash picked up.
- Provide an equal number of items for each team. The first to collect all of their items wins the round.
- Trash collectors are only allowed to throw the objects from where they are picked up. I only do this one when I have soft objects as obstacles.

ADDITIONAL **I**DEAS:

SECTION THREE

initiative elements

THOUGHTS · NOTES · REVELATIONS

Initiative Elements are interrelated to initiative games; the processing objective is the same. The only difference is that elements are constructed props which require the players to move up away from the comfort of solid ground - either by being lifted or by stepping up onto an element. These elements require a group's combined physical and/or mental effort to arrive at a solution to a presented problem. These props can be purchased or built by individuals interested in starting an experiential program or used to diversify a program already established. All necessary construction plans for the props are provided.

The elements that are suggested here are portable in nature. Materials needed, such as lumber, rope, and other supplies can be found at a local hardware store, lumber yard, or an outdoor recreation store that carries rock climbing supplies. If you run into difficulty finding the supplies I have listed, be creative with what you can find.

There are several companies who specialize in the construction of ropes courses. These companies can build permanent low and high course elements as well as portable ones (see Appendix). **I do not recommend that you build your own permanent course without qualified assistance. There are established standards in the field of ropes course construction that you would need to understand in order to avoid costly liabilities. It would be safest to leave the technical building to the experienced professionals.**

Having a variety of challenging portable elements at your disposal will expand your programming options. You can plan for indoor or outdoor use, day or evening programs. You could even travel to different sites with these elements and provide programs for more groups.

If you haven't done so already, please read through the **Initiative Games Introduction** (p. 7) the **Facilitation & Processing** (p. 2) information, and the **Spotting** (p. 116) procedures presented earlier. It will be very important to have an understanding of this information before moving on.

These elements are the tools you can work with to build interest and participation in experiential education. However, it will be the facilitation that will water the seeds of learning. The information in this section is meant to serve as a guide and does not take the place of professional training. Take every opportunity to learn from learned facilitators. There is a listing of companies who provide first rate experiential training in the Appendix section.

Remember that safety is always first. If the group is not safe with the props made available to them, move on to a different activity without props. There are a number of Initiative Games that can accomplish similar objectives. Stay safe and have fun!

THOUGHTS · NOTES · REVELATIONS

QUAD JAM

Thanks to Craig Dobkin as written by Karl Rohnke in "Bottomless Baggie."

NEEDS: 4 - 4" x 4" x 8' boards (from **Friendship Walk**).

PROCEDURE: Set out the boards in a square shape. This square can accommodate about 5 or 6 participants per board. Ask the players to split themselves into 4 even groups. Then ask each group to stand behind one of the boards - along the side facing in toward the center. At this point I go with the following progression until I feel the group has reached its challenge level.

Challenge 1: Everyone stand up, with both feet on the boards for a count of 6 seconds. (Sounds easy doesn't it?!) "Want another challenge?"

Challenge 2: Walking on top of the boards, circle the square and return to your starting position - without stepping off the boards. Any steps off the board and the entire group starts over. "Want another challenge?"

Challenge 3: Ask each player to look, and point, at the spot on the board directly across from them. Then ask each player to get to that spot without touching the ground. (Most groups think they just have to walk around the circle, but.... Here's where we hope to see some helping happen - if it already hasn't.) "Want another challenge?"

Challenge 4: Give each board a number in clockwise order, ask groups on boards 1 and 2 to switch boards and end up in exact order on the new board. Ask 3 and 4 to do the same. "Want another challenge?"

Challenge 5: Have the groups on boards 2 and 4, 1 and 3 change. End up in the same order on the new board. (This one is interesting, because the solution is just walking around the boards again, but many groups get stuck in the mental model of doing it like the last challenge. Fun to talk about!) "Want another challenge?"

Challenge 6: Blindfold every other player, then move around the square to end up in each player's starting position. "And another?"

Challenge 7: Blindfold all players and move around one board.

129

FACILITATION/SAFETY:
- Make sure the area around the square is free of obstacles.
- Do your best to set the boards in a flat area. A little wobble does add to the adventure however.

Spotting is not a major issue for this one. In most cases participants are good about stepping down. When they progress into the higher challenges, it is good to watch the corners as they help each other around. I tend to keep reminding them to just step down if they are going to fall.

OBSERVATIONS/QUESTIONS:
- What was hard about the activity you tried? What made it easier?
- What happened when someone started to fall?
- Could falls have been prevented? How?
- How did you help the group during the activity?
- Is it hard for you to ask for help? To give help? Why do you think...?
- Is it okay to ask for help?
- What did you observe during the activity?
- Who can remember what was going through your mind during the activity?
- How did you solve challenge 5? Was there another way?
- What does it mean to "think before you act?" How would this help you in the future?

(other) •

•

VARIATIONS:
- There's a good level progression for this one. For the first level you could use a large rope square on the ground or masking tape square. Players must have both feet touching the rope or tape whenever both feet are on the ground. Try some of the first challenges at this level. The next level can be just the boards discussed above. A third level can be made by bolting a box (see **Roof Tops**) to the end of each board with a 5/8" x 5 1/2" carriage bolt (see diagram at the top of the next page). Once they have learned the skills at a lower level, they should be able to perform them at a higher level - shouldn't they?

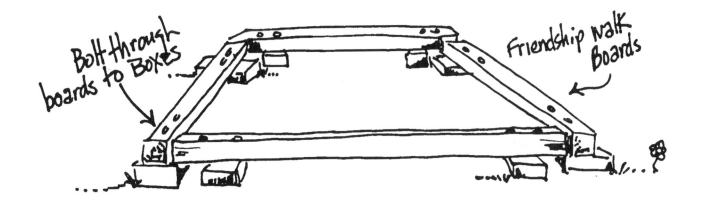

• If I have time, I like to add this introduction activity before I start the challenges. I've seen Craig Dobkin use this set up as a recognition activity. All the participants stand on the ground around the square. One at a time a player stands up on the board in front of him/her, states their name and shares a positive characteristic about themselves. (I've tried this with youth groups and have found that many have trouble stepping in and up from the group.)

• Try any of the suggested challenges non-verbally.

• For smaller groups you could use the 6' Trolleys or just 3 - 8' boards. (Using 3 - 8' boards makes the corner transitions a bit easier also.)

• As mentioned in the **Blind Beam** initiative, you could use 4" x 4" white vinyl fence posts found in the lawn and garden section of those big hardware stores. I've only seen 6' so far, so this may limit your group size - or you could be creative.

• Here's an interesting and fun mental challenge that was discovered at an Affordable Portables workshop. (Shortly after the discovery, The Movable Martini puzzle showed up in Karl Rohnke's, "FUNN Stuff Vol. 2.") Set up your 4 - 4" x 4" x 8' boards in the Martini Glass shape shown on the following page. Put a red ball, for the cherry, inside the glass (or a few balls as ice cubes). Now have your group stand up on the boards with an equal number of players on each board. The challenge, without stepping off the boards, is to move the cherry outside the glass without moving the cherry, moving as few boards as possible, and ending up with the glass in tact. Only 2 boards need to be moved to solve the puzzle. If they solve it with 3, challenge them to solve it with less than 3. (If someone knows the answer up front, ask them to remain an active observer during the process.) This is a great metaphorical activity of trying to solve a problem when you're on top of it - without looking at the problem from other points of view.

ADDITIONAL IDEAS:

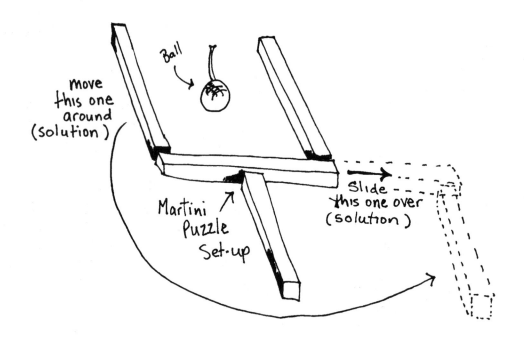

move
this one
around
(Solution)

Ball

Martini
Puzzle
Set-up

Slide
this one over
(solution)

NEEDS: Use the 12 Boxes constructed for the **Roof Tops** element. (If you don't have these Boxes, see Variations below for other options.)

PROCEDURE: Each member of the group is asked to obtain a Box from a pile of Boxes near the activity area. (I like the group to design their own structure. However, I have set the Boxes in a circle shape to save some time for other activities.) The objective for each player, after everyone is standing up on the Boxes, will be to touch each person's Box, feet only, without touching the ground in the process. The entire group must start over if someone touches the ground.

I will ask the group to create a structure that will allow the entire group to touch the tops of each Box without touching the ground. This adds another problem-solving component to the problem.

FACILITATION/**S**AFETY:
  •Ensure that the Boxes are used safely.
  •Let the group be responsible for calling touches.
  •Present the problem and answer questions before the group begins.

This is a fairly safe activity during the first phase. Do not let participants grab another participant around the neck. After each participant has touched each box without touching the ground, I process a little, then ask if they would like another challenge, using the Variations below. When they get down to a 1:2 ratio, Box to participants, do some goal setting before they start. Not many groups are successful at this stage, so you might want to encourage an attainable goal.

OBSERVATIONS/**Q**UESTIONS:
    •What type of planning occurred?
    •What is a structure?
    •Who took a leadership role?
    •How were the touches monitored? Who should be responsible for rules?
    •What was the reaction to the consequence? How was the person treated?
    •What was the reaction to fewer boxes?
    •What kind of support was taking place? Who was helping? Who wasn't?
    •Who avoided help from others? Why do you think that was?
    •Was there reaction to proximity with each other?
    •What was the success factor? Who feels successful?
(other) •
       •

VARIATIONS:

- For a very low risk variation, use pieces of 8 1/2" x 11" paper. Touching the ground is optional - it's very hard to stand on your toes for very long.
- For the next progression from paper, cut yourself some boards. I like to use the 2" x 8" x 12" size with nicely sanded corners.
- I was really intrigued by this variation. Landscaping timbers (these are 4" x 4"s with rounded edges) were cut into various sizes. These boards were set on their sides for the first round of the initiative. The next step was to have players, without touching the ground, tip the boards on end and stand on top. Very interesting.
- Offer blindfolds to volunteers.
- Progressively take away boxes (2 at a time, no blindfolds).
- Provide a rhythmic song to the movement.
- Move into **Box Top**, from this activity.

ADDITIONAL **I**DEAS:

NEEDS: Several Boxes from **Roof Tops** element or construct a Box Top element as shown in the diagram.

TASK: How many group members can be on the platform for 5 seconds without touching the ground? (Sing a round of Row-Row-Row your boat if it fits with the story.) There is usually no consequence for this activity, it is more of a "try it till you get it or settle for it" activity.

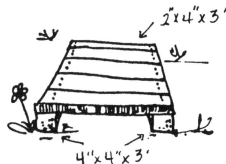

FACILITATION/SAFETY:
- Ensure that the Boxes are set firm in relation to the ground.
- Check the Boxes for defects and weakness.
- Check surrounding area for unsafe objects.
- Present problem and safety. Answer questions before group begins.

The ideal situation here is to have someone spotting at every corner. If this is not possible, the facilitator must continuously circle the element and spot. Do not allow participants to grab around the neck or pile on top of each other. All participants must have at least one foot touching a Box/Board. It is critical here for participants to step off, when falling, without pulling the other group members off with them. If participants become unsafe, move to another activity.

OBSERVATIONS/QUESTIONS:
- What kind of planning took place?
- Was there a leader?
- Who participated? Who hung back?
- What was the reaction to personal space?
- Was there concern for others' physical comfort?
- Was anyone being unhelpful? How does that affect the task?
- What was the fun factor?
- How successful were you?

(other) •
     •

VARIATIONS:
- How many feet can the group get on the Boxes/Boards? (What if they weren't standing?)
- You could use masking tape to form a box on the floor.
- Develop a strategy and then try it non-verbally.
- Progress to this activity from **Lilly Pads & Islands** or **Box Hop**.

ADDITIONAL **I**DEAS:

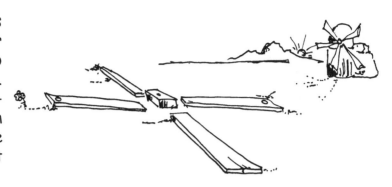

NEEDS: 4 - 2" x 8" x 5' boards and 1 Box (see **Roof Tops** for Box description). Refer to diagram for set-up reference. If the surface you are working on is slippery, use foam cupboard lining under the boards (this can be found at a Wal-mart type store).

TASK: Evenly distribute group members on each one of the boards before you give the directions. When the group is ready for instructions, present the problem. (This activity with all 4 boards is best with a group of 16 to 24 players. If you have a smaller group, see the Variations below.)

Have each player notice the position he/she is standing in on their board. (i.e., first position, second, middle, last, whatever it may be). The challenge is to:
1) Change boards without touching the ground.
2) Touch the Box in the center, with both feet at the same time, before touching any other board.
3) You should end up on a new board in your original position without any of your original "Board Members." (This rule only works with groups of 12 or less. If you have more, try no more than one original board member.)
Consequence should fit the level of challenge. The person who touches starts over, is blindfolded, or everyone starts over.

FACILITATION/SAFETY:
•Ensure that the boards are on a level surface.
•Set the group up on the boards before giving directions.
•Present problem and answer questions before the group begins.
•One foot must be in contact with a board or the Box at all times (this is supposed to prevent jumping).
•Have the group tell you when they are ready to start the activity.
•Let the group call the touches.

This is a fairly low risk activity when done with the boards. More spotting is required on narrower and elevated variations. Spot when 2 people are moving around each other. Make sure the area around the element is free of obstacles. Encourage the group members to step off the boards if they are falling without pulling other members off the boards. Do not allow participants to grab another participant around the neck or ride piggy-back during this activity.

The most interesting part for me has always been watching the planning phase of this activity. How effective is the planning when they are all standing on their boards? I have "set them up" in this way to see if they will get off the boards and assemble in a more user-friendly planning formation. This adds great potential to the processing.

OBSERVATIONS/QUESTIONS:

- What sort of planning occurred? Where did it take place? (Did the group stay on the boards to plan or take some other shape?)
- What assumptions were made during the activity?
- What occurred with players in relation to where they were on the boards?
- What kind of support was going on? Who was being helpful?
- Were there some people who didn't want help? Was this okay?
- Did teamwork take place? In what ways?
- Who took responsibility for touches? How did the group react?
- What were the reactions to being helped?..being close together?
- What does it take to be successful?
- Did gender play a part in this activity? (with mixed groups)

(other) •

•

VARIATIONS:

- If you have less than 16 players, take away a board or two.
- **Traffic Jam** - stick a player (leader) on the Box and have this person give all the directions for movement.
- One of my favorites on a hot day is to do this activity with every player carrying a full cup of water (no drinking until the end).
- Do the activity on 4" x 4" x 6' boards used in **Quad Jam**.
- For an indoor low cost **Windmill**, use masking tape on the floor. Tape out the size of each board around a center box (made of tape).
- The **Windmill** is similar to the "TP Shuffle" in Karl Rohnke's book, "Silver Bullets," p. 110. Pick up any one of Karl's other books and you'll find other variations to this activity as well. All you need are the boards from **Windmill**.

ADDITIONAL IDEAS:

OPPOSITES ATTRACT

NEEDS: Three old car tires (2 identical - like whitewalls), and 1 - 2" x 8" x 5' board (as used in **Windmill** or **Mountain Tops**). Provide a section of old rope or webbing if the group chooses to use it to move tires. Also, a nice open area about 30' long.

PROCEDURE: The entire group, at the same time, must progress across a 30' expanse using the supplied equipment without touching the ground. (A group of more than 12 will need additional equipment.) The board or participants are not allowed to touch <u>two like tires</u> at the same time, or touch the ground within the expanse. The webbing or rope is supplied for the strict use of moving a tire. The consequences of touching should fit the level of challenge: blindfold touchers or have the group start over.

FACILITATION/SAFETY:
- Check board for sliver potential; sand board if needed.
- Check area for dangers a player may fall on.
- Do not allow individuals with back problems to move tires.
- Be aware of teeter affect with board on one tire.
- Present problem and allow time for questions before group begins.

You will want to spot around the board at all times. Require that participants have at least one foot on a board or a tire at all times. Take special care when the board is balancing on one tire. Continue to warn about pinched fingers and toes. Watch for proper manipulation of the tires; lift with the legs not the back, or pull with the webbing or rope. Do not allow any long distance jumping or shoulder sitting.

OBSERVATIONS/QUESTIONS:
- Was there any planning involved?
- Who shared ideas? Who had ideas but didn't share? Why?
- Did the group use all the resources?
- How did the group support each other?
- Who was doing the work during the activity?
- What made the activity easy? Or hard to do?
- What was the reaction to touches?
- Were blindfolded players taken care of?
- What was the level of success?

(other) •
  •

VARIATIONS:
•Pair up players. One person is blindfolded, the other the caretaker.

ADDITIONAL IDEAS:

NEEDS: Two 2" x 8" x 5' boards (from **Flip Flop** element) and 6 wooden platform sections. Each section is made with 3 - 2" x 6" x 4' boards attached to 2" x 4" braces (see diagram). Two 5/8" holes are drilled to accommodate the attachment of two "Boxes" (Box construction found in **Roof Tops** element). Use 3 sections together for the first platform, 2 for the second, and 1 for the third (3 **Mountain Tops**). Each Mountain Top should be 6' away from another.

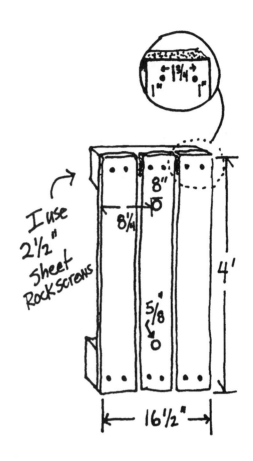

I use 2½" Sheet Rock screws

PROCEDURE: The group of 8 - 12 must progress from the largest platform to the smallest without any person or boards touching the ground. The entire group must be standing on the first platform when ready to begin. Each person must have <u>one foot on wood at all times</u> (this prevents jumping). Consequences should fit level of challenge. Any touches, the person starts over, group starts over or person is blindfolded.

FACILITATION/SAFETY:
- Ensure all platforms are safe and stable (not wobbly).
- Check boards for cracks and/or splinters.
- Clear area of all hazards.
- Instruct participants to step down if falling, without pulling others.
- Present the problem and answer questions before the group begins.

There is a lot to be aware of during this activity. Extra staff on this one helps. Spotters should be at the corners of the platform when a majority of the group is on it. Spot other platforms as needed. Always spot person walking across the board. If there are not enough spotters, continuously circle the platforms. Monitor the safe use of the boards so fingers and toes are not pinched and people are not knocked off. Do not allow the boards to be thrown to others. Movements should be controlled so boards do not slip sideways. Stop to evaluate activity when things become chaotic. Avoid this activity if the platforms are too wet.

OBSERVATIONS/QUESTIONS:

- Where and how did ideas come about? Were they listened to?
- How comfortable were participants during activity? Did that change?
- What type of leadership took place?
- What type of support was offered by non-active participants?
- Was there any reaction to touching the ground?
- How was frustration handled?
- What happened to the energy level as the activity progressed?
- Was the group having success? Did they see that?

(other) •

   •

VARIATIONS:

- Some players carry a glass or bucket of water.
- Everyone wears a small day pack.
- Whoever is touching a board that touches the ground is blindfolded.

ADDITIONAL IDEAS:

SWAMP WALK
From the Meuse, Karl Rohnke, "The Bottomless Bag Again".

NEEDS: 10 "Boxes" as described in **Roof Tops**. 2 to 4 boards - 4" x 4" x 8' long (used in **Friendship Walk**) <u>or</u> the 2" x 8" x 5' boards from **Windmill**. 20' of old webbing or rope.

PROCEDURE: Use the diagram provided for the set up. The group must progress from one end of the swamp to the other, using only the resources provided (4 boards is easier, 2 is the hardest and most time consuming). People and resources (depending how it is presented) are not allowed to touch the ground within the swamp. Consequences of touching should match level of ability (i.e., being blindfolded, loss of a board, starting over).

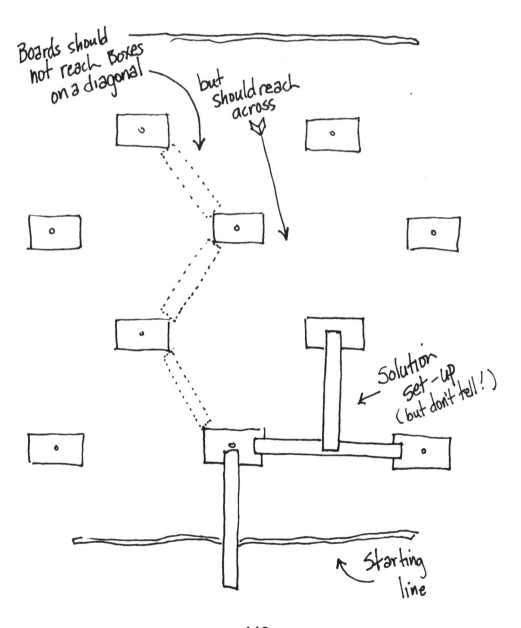

Boards should not reach Boxes on a diagonal

but should reach across

Solution set-up (but don't tell!)

Starting line

143

FACILITATION/SAFETY:

•Set up activity on an even surface (does not need to be level).
•Check all boards and Boxes for cracks that may cause problems.
•Provide more boards for lower functioning (4), less for higher (2).
•Provide a long piece of webbing for lowering boards.
•Board placements must always overlap at least 3" (4 fingers).
•Present the problem and answer questions before the group begins.

The only major safety concern here is board movement. Do not allow boards to be dropped or thrown. Require that the webbing be used at all times when lowering boards. This is especially important when group members have back problem history. Make sure Boxes are solidly balanced on the ground. Spot challenged individuals (i.e., blindfolded) when crossing boards. Do not allow individuals to jump or carry each other. "Remember, placement of the Boxes is key to making this initiative problem work. Spend time before the (group) shows up, making sure that the 'islands' are in a functional position" (Rohnke, p.112).

OBSERVATIONS/QUESTIONS:

•What type of leadership evolved? Who was involved?
•What level of involvement was taking place by each member?
•Where were ideas coming from? Were they heard?
•How did individuals handle "waiting?"
•How was frustration dealt with?
•Were challenged members taken care of?
•What changes were made along the way? Who encouraged them?
•How did the group handle less boards? Props?

(other) •

    •

VARIATIONS:

•Group must bring a large (light weight) barrel with them.
•Each group member carries a cup of water across boards.
•Eliminate boards after the main problem is solved (no less than 2).
•A very interesting variation suggested for corporate groups in the, "Book of Metaphors, Volume II," by Michael Gass, involves a different set up. "The blocks (Boxes) are placed closer together at the 'starting' side of the swamp and gradually farther apart as the group progresses to the 'finish' side." The short version: the first two rows of Boxes can be reached by placing boards at an angle to the next row. The second and third rows are set up so the "T"

solution works. The third and fourth rows are too far for the "T" solution - another solution must be found. The metaphor being: How do we adapt to changes in the workplace. I highly recommend picking up a copy of Mr. Gass' book.

ADDITIONAL **I**DEAS:

Thanks to Karl Rohnke, "The Bottomless Bag Again."

NEEDS: Four separate 4" x 4" x 6' boards. Holes (5/8") are drilled in each board 12" apart. These holes accommodate ropes 4' in length. I like to cut up old climbing rope. It's easy on the hands, and it lasts a long time. Each board has eye bolts screwed into the ends so that 2 boards can be connected together to form 1 long Trolley for 12 people. If you can avoid tying knots in the rope ends, more variations (see Variation section) are available. (See construction diagram below.)

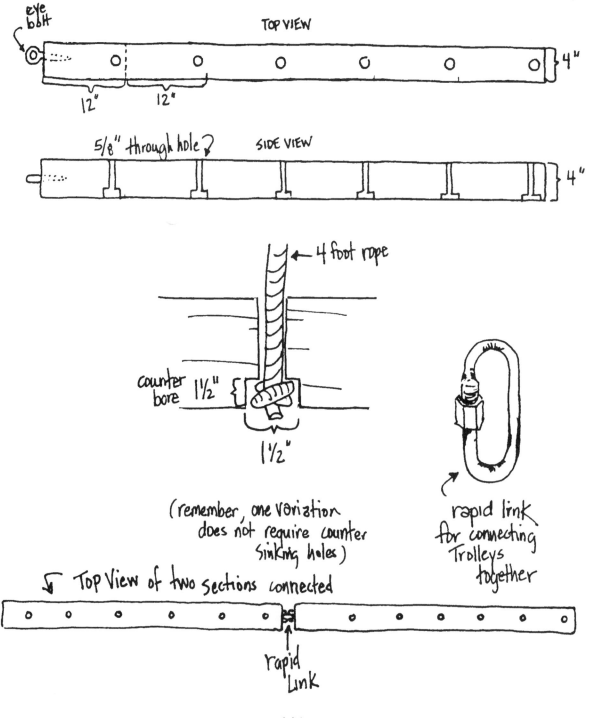

PROCEDURE: Using the Trolleys, the group must cross a designated area with only the boards touching the ground. Consequences for touching should fit the level of ability - blindfold, loss of rope, start over, turn around, etc.

FACILITATION/SAFETY:
- Check for uneven ground and any obstacles that may cause tipping.
- Check all rope-to-wood contact for good knots.
- Ropes should be long enough to prevent back discomfort.
- This is not a speed event. Speed increases falling potential.
- Present the problem and answer questions before the group begins.

Part of the problem is for the group to figure out how to use the Trolleys. Karl suggests to "just throw them down or cross them so that their position doesn't indicate possible usage" (p. 222). I like to let 2 small groups work separately before providing the rapid links to connect boards together making 1 large group. For added adventure, have participants connect boards without getting off.

This event often causes a "domino effect" type fall. More often than not, it is a forward fall. One spotter should be on each end of the Trolleys if the potential for falling is great (younger groups fall more). Encourage participants to let go of the ropes and step off if they start to fall. Extra attention should be given to challenged participants (i.e. blindfolded, backwards, no ropes).

OBSERVATIONS/QUESTIONS:
- Did this become a race between the 2 sets of Trolleys?
- Was competition a factor?
- Who became the leaders, and how did it change when connected?
- Why was leadership important?
- How were they communicating?
- How was frustration handled?
- How did the physical challenge affect performance?
- What was the focus during times of failure?
- What type of success did the group acknowledge?

(other) •
        •

VARIATIONS:
- •Eliminate all ropes except for the front and back ropes.
- •Have the group move backwards.
- •Don't countersink holes for this variation. I use old climbing rope cut in 4' lengths with a rope cutter. I don't put the ropes in the wood or knots in the ropes, I just set everything down and tell them to cross a span. The only thing that can touch the span is the wood, and each rope supplied must be used to aid the crossing. (Rope has to be strung through the holes from alternating sides to keep the board from flipping.)
- •Karl Rohnke does a **Trolleys**-like activity using balloons. Have each player blow up a big balloon. Working in small groups, have players line up and put a balloon between each person near the belly-button area. Now walk around without dropping any balloons. After some practice, put small groups together to form bigger groups. I like to end up in a big circle walking clockwise. For the finale I ask the group to stop walking. Then I ask them to move in toward the center as far as they can without losing any balloons. "Fire in the hole!"
- •Take those long foam noodle pool toys, cut them in half. Place a noodle, the long way, between players and walk around this way without dropping the noodle. (For a bunch of colorful fun, pick up a copy of "50 Ways to Use Your Noodle" by Cavert & Sikes. It has 30 different land games and 20 problem-solving activities.)
- •This one is very interesting and a bit safer. Get 4 long sections of climbing rope to substitute for the boards. Provide the 4' hand ropes. Ask the group to construct an apparatus that they can manipulate from point "A" to point "B." Each foot of each player must be in contact with rope at all times or suffer the sting of a _____ fish.
- •Use the Trolley boards to do the Martini Puzzle described in the **Quad Jam** variation section.

ADDITIONAL **I**DEAS:

NEEDS: Four 4" x 4" x 8' boards, 2 - 4" x 4" x 2' boards, 2 - 13' sections of 1" tubular webbing, 2 - 3' sections of 1" tubular webbing, 2 rag rugs - 2' x 3 1/2', 8 rapid links, 8 - 1/2" x 4' eye bolts, nuts and washers, 8 - 1/2" x 7" through bolts with nuts and washers, and a medium-size open area. Set up the element according to the diagram below.

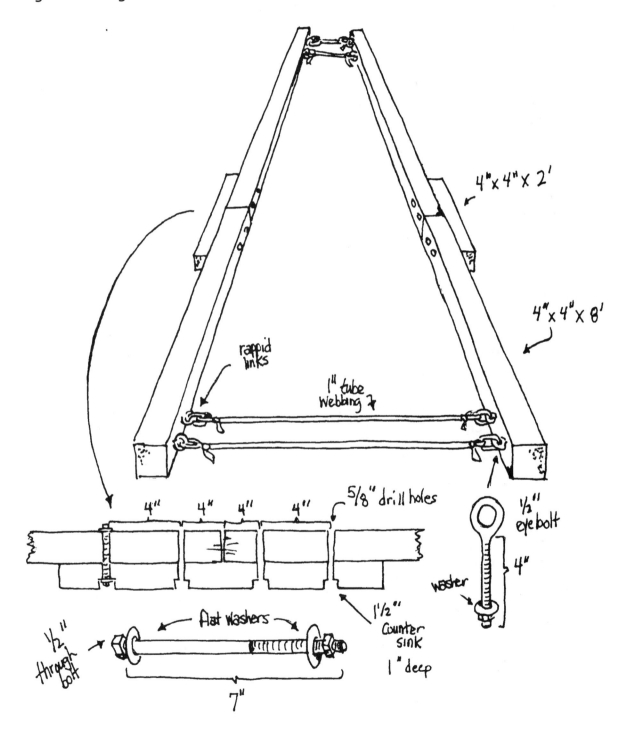

PROCEDURE: Group members will work in pairs to see how far they can progress down the element from the narrow to the wide end. Pairs must stay in contact with each other at all times while staying on their own section of the element.

FACILITATION/**S**AFETY:
- Do not allow pairs to lock fingers together "Roman knuckle" style.
- Provide adequate spotting during the entire activity (see below).
- Present the problem, and answer questions before the group begins.

This is a high level trust activity if the boards are really far apart. (The **Friendship Walk** is a portable version of the classic, Wild Woosey low ropes element. Instead of boards, it's loosey goosey wires.) The challenge occurs at the wide end when participants must lean in and support (commit to) each other to progress.

Spotting during this activity is most important. Two Spotters (S's) should be assigned to each Active Participant (AP) before he/she steps up onto the element. S's spot at each side of the AP's. As the AP's move farther down the span, spotting rugs can be placed underneath the AP's. S's hold a ragrug under the AP to support a fall if taken. S's, as always, must pay attention. A good grip on the rugs is necessary. Keep the rug up close to the AP's, without holding them up, so if there is a fall the AP will not jerk the rug out of a S's hands. In every case I've seen so far, since the element is close to the ground, the AP's are able to just step out of a fall. However, if you choose to spread the element out really far, spotting rugs will be very important. Provide a good spotting demonstration before starting. I let participants choose partners for this element, unless there are 2 participants that I want to see working together. Before starting, gather everyone around and ask for input about characteristics of friendships. Support, trust, and being there for you, are just some of the characteristics that come up. I ask the participants to keep these characteristics in mind as they try this element.

OBSERVATIONS/**Q**UESTIONS:
- What was the experience like for you?
- How well do you think you and your partner worked together?
- What made the activity difficult? What made it easy?
- What characteristics of friendship did you use during the activity?
- What does it take to travel down the span?
- Did you feel that you were successful? In what ways?
- What do you think it would take to be more successful?

(other) •

•

VARIATIONS:

   •**Group Walk**. What are the characteristics of a group? Remember these as you attempt this next task. Have the group do the walk together. When a player steps on a board, they must be in contact with a player from the other board. As players are added, the same rule applies with each addition. All participants on the boards must be in contact in such a way that if an electrical impulse was started with one player, it would go through all the players on the boards. Set the boards far enough apart at the wide end to get some leaning going, but not so far that it would require spotting rugs.

ADDITIONAL **I**DEAS:

NEEDS: You'll need 2 - Tamper Poles (from **Electric Amoeba** or **The Web**), a Hula-Hoop, 4 - bungee cords (from **Bun-G-Box:** if you do the PVC Box version, then you will want to get some pre-fab cords with the hooks on the ends for **Electric Portal**), 2 - sturdy milk crates, 2 - 2" x 10" x 5' boards (from **Windmill**), 1 - 4" x 4" x 6' board (from **Trolleys**) and 2 boundary line markers - ropes or webbing (see Diagram below for set up).

Set the Hula-Hoop up so that the bottom is 9" from the ground (consider that a larger Hoop will make the activity easier). The boundary lines should extend parallel to the hoop 3' on either side. This will leave a 6' span to travel across.

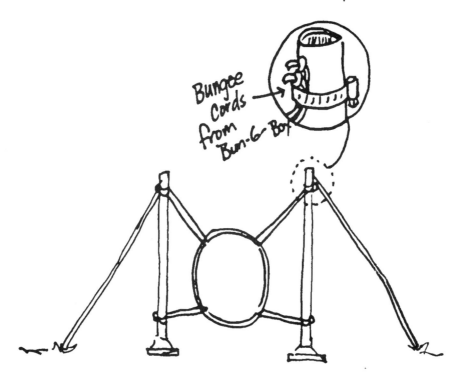

PROCEDURE: The group, starting on one side, will need to pass through the Portal (Hoop) without touching the 6' span or any part of the Portal structure.

FACILITATION/SAFETY:
- Inspect all equipment for damage that may result in failure.
- None of the resources should be thrown.
- No other resource can be used.
- Present the problem and answer questions before the group begins.

This is a very challenging activity and often takes quite a bit of time. However, it can be done. I will leave it up to you and your groups to figure it out.

OBSERVATIONS/**Q**UESTIONS:
- What sorts of ideas were shared? What ideas were not? Why?
- Who took a leadership role initially? Who ended up as the leader?
- What was most frustrating about the activity?
- How were you able to overcome the frustration? (if at all)
- What were some of the internal thoughts going on during the action?
- Were any of you apprehensive about crossing over the boards? Why?
- What level of trust was involved?
- Are there some people you trust more than others? Why?
- What are some qualities of trust?

(other) •

•

VARIATIONS:

ADDITIONAL **I**DEAS:

NEEDS: **The Web** is a series of small strings woven between a larger rope frame (I use 3/8" rope), leaving 12 to 18 large openings. You will need 4 - 2" hose clamps to fit on the Tamper Poles (described in **Electric Amoeba**). These clamps hold the rope to the poles (see diagram). It will also be helpful to guy the poles out to the sides. I tie some extra rope around the top of the pole and then down to a gallon jug of water at each side (see diagram below).

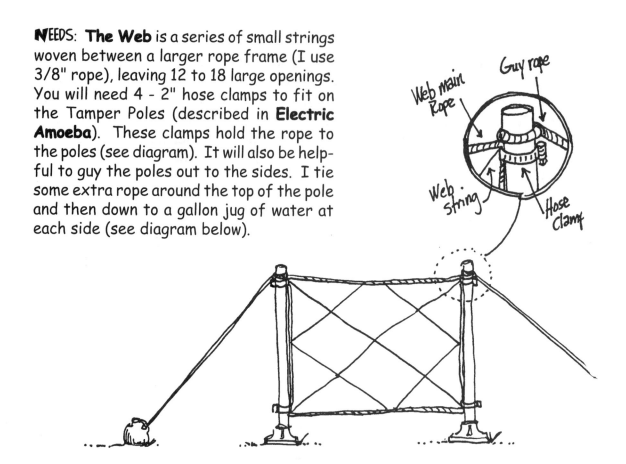

PROCEDURE: Pass each participating member through a separate web opening without letting any body part touch the web (string). Once an opening is used, it is closed to further passage. Participants may not be passed over or under the web. Consequences should fit level of challenge. Anyone who touches, starts over, is blindfolded, loses an opening, and/or the group starts over. It is important to lead into **The Web** with a lifting activity of some type.

FACILITATION/SAFETY:
   •Review spotting and lifting procedures (see, Safety First section).
   •Let the group members call touches.
   •First participant must go through feet first, stomach down.
   •Web should not be higher than tallest participant.
   •Present problem, and answer questions before group begins.

Take some time to discuss the importance of safety before starting the activity. Ask individuals to spot at all times, even if they are not touching the person. Direct them never to "just let go" of a participant because he or she touched the web. Do not allow participants to dive through the holes. Provide extra spotting around the head and the neck.

Please keep in mind here that this is a very brief description of an activity that has a high level of risk. Again, I encourage you to have a good feeling for experiential exercises before presenting these types of activities. You do not want to exceed the challenge and safety level of your group.

OBSERVATIONS/**Q**UESTIONS:
- What type of planning took place? Who was involved?
- What reactions surfaced while being passed through? Did you feel safe?
- How did support come about in the group?
- Did anyone ask for anything from the group?
- What were the levels of involvement from individuals?
- What factors determined group order? Was gender or ability considered?
- What was the level of quality during the activity?
- How did the group determine success?

(other) •

 •

VARIATIONS:
- Start half of the group on either side, then switch sides going through the web.
- Re-open hole by selling physical challenges - i.e., blindfolded.
- Set a limit of touches when the group must start over.
- Here is one I discovered to be very interesting. Set up the 2 Tampers about 5' apart - by themselves. Gather the group on one side of the Tampers. Provide the group with a roll of masking tape and then present them with some or all of these challenges:

  1) With the Tampers being the sides of an opening, create the top and bottom of an opening that all the group members can pass through. You have 5 minutes.

  2) With the Tampers as sides, create the top and bottom of the smallest opening that all the group members can get through. You have 7 minutes and whatever time was left from the first challenge.

  3) Move the same opening to a different part of the Tampers. You have 10 minutes and whatever time is left from the last 2 challenges.

  4) Using the Tampers as the sides, and the ground as the bottom of your opening, create the closest top to the ground that your group members can go under. You have whatever minutes are left from the last 3 challenges.

155

Keep in mind all the safety issues mentioned for **The Web**. I like this one because the group is allowed to choose their own level of challenge.

ADDITIONAL **I**DEAS:

THE CUBE

Thanks to Earl LaBlanc.

NEEDS: You will find all this interesting stuff in the plumbing and sprinkler system sections of a good-sized hardware store. I'm going to give you the names for the pieces, from there you're on your own. Remember, when in doubt, be creative.

After talking with Earl, we both came up with this same system (if you discover a better way, for the same or less money, let us know). **The Cube** I use has 2 1/2' sides (Earl likes to use 3' sides - you can decide what works for you). You will need 8 sections of 3/4" x 2 1/2' PVC (this is 2 - 10' lengths cut into 4 pieces), 8 Side Outs, 3/4" x 3/4" x 1/2" (these are the corners that the PVC and the threaded risers fit into), 12 - 1/2" x 10" threaded PVC Risers (I found these in the sprinkler section. I've only seen them in black.), and 8 - 1/2" threaded couplings to connect the risers together. This makes the Cube. You will also need something to hang it up, like a rope or section of bungee cord (I use the one I have for the **Electric Amoeba**).

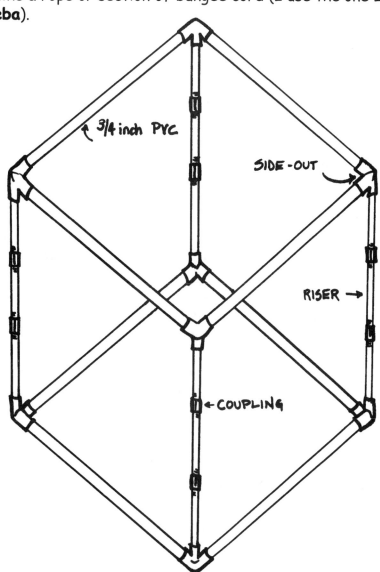

PROCEDURE: Assemble your Cube (see diagram on previous page for a visual). To ensure the Cube stays together after I hang it, I cut up rubber bands and stick a piece in between each connection - this holds it together nice and tight. Hang this Cube 2' to 3' above the ground, depending on the challenge you want. Now you're ready to go.

The idea behind **The Cube** is similar to **The Web**. Each member of the group will go through the Cube entering one hole and exiting another without moving the structure (or if you can hang a bell off of it - without ringing the bell). If the Cube is moved, the entrance/exit pattern is closed. Keep this in mind - there are 5 exits for every entrance. There are 6 entrances. This makes 30 patterns to choose from. If you want to limit the patterns, just designate a few sides as entrances.

FACILITATION/**S**AFETY:
- •Review spotting and lifting procedures (see Safety First section).
- •Inspect surroundings for hazards (i.e., tree limbs, rocks, & sticks).
- •Let the group members be responsible for Cube movements.
- •At no time should a participant's head be lower than their knees. (We don't want to see any human lawn darts!)
- •The Cube should be no higher than the tallest participant's shoulders.
- •Present problem, and answer questions before group begins.

Just as in **The Web**, take some time to discuss the importance of safety before starting the activity. Ask individuals to spot at all times, even if they are not touching the person. Direct them never to "just let go" of a participant because he/she moved the Cube. Do not allow participants to dive through the holes. Always provide extra spotting around the head and the neck.

Lifting activities are considered high risk to most participants and facilitators. Keep a watchful eye on all movements and stop all unsafe actions.

More often than not, I will provide paper and pencil to the group so they can keep track of combinations. I've also gone to marking the corner pieces with numbers for each opening - but a challenge is a challenge.

OBSERVATIONS/**Q**UESTIONS:
- •What were some of the issues we had to consider before we even started this activity?
- •What type of planning takes/took place? Who was involved?
- •What reactions surfaced while being passed through the Cube?

•How is/was the safety level? Did you feel safe?
•How did support come about in the group?
•Did anyone ask for anything from the group?
•What were the levels of involvement from individuals?
•Is/was everyone involved in the spotting? Why?
•What system was used to keep track of entrance/exit combinations?
•What factors determined group order? Was gender or ability considered?
•What was the level of quality during the activity?
•How does the group determine success?

(other) •

•

VARIATIONS:

•For a less-lifting variation, have 2 players hold the Cube. These players are allowed to move the Cube in any way to help their team members go through. The Cube cannot touch the ground nor can it touch a player who is not holding the Cube. Make sure you change holders so they can go through also.
•You could make a Cube out of hula-hoops by taping the touching edges. Hang it from one of the sides instead of the corner.

ADDITIONAL IDEAS:

NEEDS: Different lengths of 4" x 4" boards from other elements (I use 2 **Trolley** boards and the 4 **Blind Beam** boards) are supported by the Boxes - you'll need 12 (see diagram below), platforms of different sizes (from **Mountain Tops**) or the webbing circles from **Raccoon Circles**, and a large flat open area.

PROCEDURE: I like to set my **Roof Tops** in this order:
Section 1 - One **Trolleys** board, Section 2 - One **Blind Beam** board,
Section 3 - One **Trolleys** board and one **Blind Beam** board end to end (4 Boxes needed),
Section 4 - Two **Blind Beam** boards end to end (4 Boxes needed).

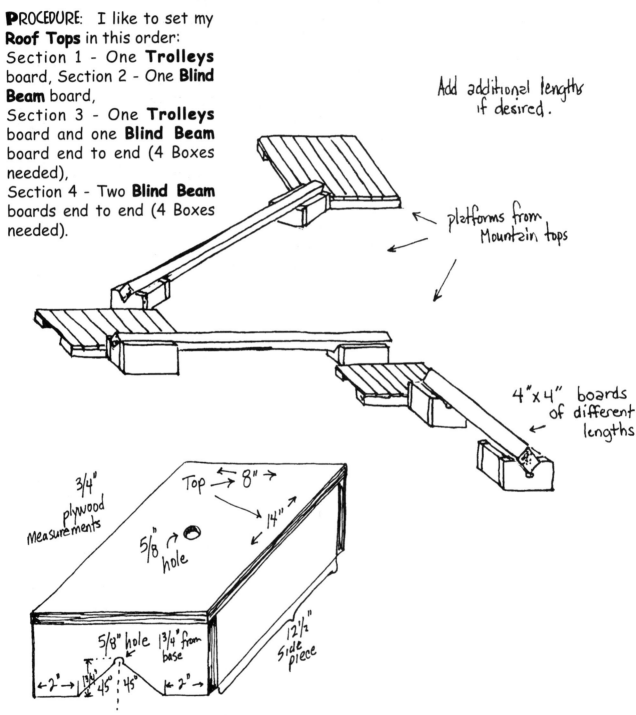

Add additional lengths if desired.

platforms from Mountain tops

4"x4" boards of different lengths

3/4" plywood measurements

Top → 8" →

14"

5/8" hole

5/8" hole 1 3/4" from base

12 1/2" side piece

←2"→ 1 3/4" 45° 45° ←2"→

Drill 5/8" hole before cutting angles.

The group begins at one end of the element (usually before the shortest length) and travels the different lengths of the element without touching the ground. For additional difficulty, do not allow participants' feet to pass or cross one another when walking the "roofs" (e. g., the right foot cannot pass the left foot). The only people that can physically assist roof walkers are the ones on a roof or platform. Consequence should fit level of difficulty. If there is a touch, individual starts from the beginning of the element, individual goes to the end of the established line of participants, or the entire group starts from the beginning.

FACILITATION/SAFETY:
- Make certain the element is assembled properly.
- Make sure element is on a flat level surface.
- Never use element when surfaces are wet.
- If Boxes are used on slick surfaces, use small squares of foam cupboard lining to prevent the Boxes from sliding.
- This is not a speed event. Speed increases falling potential.
- Ensure the area around the element is clear of obstacles.
- Present the problem, and answer questions before the group begins.

There must be adequate spotting on this activity due to its nature (please make sure you have read through the Safety First section of this book). If there are not enough extra spotters available to see a group through a section, ask group members who have reached a platform to step down and assist in spotting - not holding (they should still remember to proceed in the same order when traveling). The last section of this activity will require that most group members be on the boards. Encourage participants to step down to the ground if they are about to fall, without pulling others with them. As always, use your best judgment when it comes to safety.

OBSERVATIONS/QUESTIONS:
- What type of planning went on?
- Did participants work alone or as a team? Did this change?
- What were the reactions to falling off?
- Did anyone get discouraged? How did it affect the activity?
- What were some strengths and weaknesses in the group?
- How was the group using support?
- What was the communication like during the activity?
- Where does success come from?

(other) •
    •

161

VARIATIONS:
- Start half of the group at each end. Set up the element in a way that there are 2 short ends - at each end, then 2 mid-size with 1 long in the middle. Hopefully the groups will help each other complete the task.
- Provide safe props for an easier travel - e.g., webbing, foam bat.
- You could also have the first section board turned over on its side for a flatter and easier surface to cross (good for starting progression).

ADDITIONAL **I**DEAS:

REFERENCES

Cain, J. & Jolliff, B. (1998). *Teamwork & teamplay.* Dubuque, IA: Kendall Hunt. 800-228-0810

Cavert, C. J. & Sikes, S. (1997). *50 ways to use your noodle: Loads of land games with foam noodle toys.* Tulsa, OK: Learning Unlimited. 888-622-4203

Diamond, Lenny. 11 Sequin Rd. West Hartford, CT 06117. 603-357-2181.

Gass, M. A., (1995). *Book of metaphors.* vol. II. Dubuque, IA: Kendall Hunt. 800-228-0810

Gerstein, J. (1994). The Nurturing Spoons. *The family circuit: a newsletter on theory, research, & practice of family adventure, 2* (1), 2. (No longer in publication.)

Heider, J. (1985). *The tao of leadership.* Atlanta GA: Humanics Limited.

Johnson, D. W., & Johnson, F. P. (1991). *Joining together: Group theory and group skills.* Boston, MA: Allyn and Bacon.

Knapp, C. E. (1988). *Creating humane climates outdoors: A people skill primer.* Charleston, WV: Appalachia Educational Laboratory

Nadler, R. S., & Luckner, J. L. (1992). *Processing the adventure experience.* Dubuque, IA: Kendall Hunt. 800-228-0810

Rohnke, K. (1984). *Silver bullets.* Hamilton MA: Project Adventure.

Rohnke, K. (1989). *Cowstails and cobras II.* Hamilton, MA: Project Adventure.

Rohnke, K. (1994). *The bottomless bag again.* Dubuque, IA: Kendall/ Hunt. 800-228-0810

Rohnke, K. *Bag of tricks,* Newsletter. P.O. Box 77, Hamilton, MA 01936. (This newsletter is no longer in circulation.)

Schoel, J., Prouty, D., & Radcliffe, P. (1988). *Islands of healing: A guide to adventure based counseling.* Hamilton, MA: Project Adventure.

Senge, P. M. (1990). *The fifth discipline.* New York: Doubleday.

Sikes, S. (1998). *Executive marbles and other team building activites.* Tulsa, OK: Learning Unlimited. 888-622-4203

Sikes, S. (1995). *Feeding the zircon gorilla and other team building activities.* Tulsa, OK: Learning Unlimited. 888-622-4203

Webster, S. E. (1989). *Ropes course safety manual: An instructor's guide to initiatives, and low and high elements.* Hamilton, MA: Project Adventure.

Tom Smith - For additional information on the use of Raccoon Circles and his other activities, send Tom $10 for his packet to, Raccoon Institute, 14618 County Hwy NN, Cazemovia, Wisc., 53924.

Appendix

APPENDIX

THOUGHTS · NOTES · REVELATIONS

Corey, G., Corey, M. S., Callanan, P., & Russell, J. M. (1992). *Group techniques, 2nd edition.* Pacific Grove, CA: Brooks/Cole.

Knapp, C. E. (1992). *Lasting lessons: A teacher's guide to reflecting on experience.* Charleston, WV: Clearinghouse on Rural Education and Small Schools. (I highly recommend this one.)

Johnson, F. P., & Johnson, D. W. (1991). *Joining together: Group theory and group skills, 4th edition.* Boston, MA: Allyn and Bacon.

Nadler, R. S., & Luckner, J. L. (1992). *Processing the adventure experience.* Dubuque, IA: Kendall/Hunt.

Priest, S., Gass, M., & Gillis, L. (2000). *Essential elements of facilitation.* Dubuque, IA: Kendall/Hunt.

Schoel, J., Prouty, D., & Radcliffe. (1988). *Islands of healing: A guide to adventure based counseling.* Hamilton, MA: Project Adventure. 800-795-9039

Sugerman, D.A., & Gass, M., (2000). *Reflective learning: theory & practice.* Dubuque, IA: Kendall/Hunt.

Bacon, S. (1983). *The conscious use of metaphor in outward bound.* Denver, CO: Colorado Outward Bound School.

Newstrom, J. W., & Scannell, E. E. (1980). *Games trainers play: Experiential learning exercises.* New York: McGraw-Hill, Inc.

Newstrom, J. W., & Scannell, E. E. (1983). *More games trainers play: Experiential learning exercises.* New York: McGraw-Hill, Inc.

Priest, S., & Rohnke, K. (2000). *101 of the best corporate team building activities we know.* Dubuque, IA: Kendall/Hunt.

Priest, S., Sikes, S., & Evans, F. (2000). *99 of the best experiential corporate games we know!* Tulsa, Oklahoma: eXperientia Publication.

Rohnke, K. (1989). *Cowstails and cobras II.* Dubuque, IA: Kendall/Hunt.

Rohnke, K. (1995). *Funn stuff, Vol. 1.* Dubuque, IA: Kendall/Hunt.

Scannell, E. E., & Newstrom, J. W. (1991). *Still more games trainers play: Experiential learning exercises.* New York: McGraw-Hill, Inc.

Scott Trent. Scott has a top notch portable system of activities called *Organizational Building Blocks.* He can customize blocks with your logo. Included are over 15 activities that can be done with the blocks. Call 972-234-2725 for more information.

Trak Pak. This is a very useful processing fanny pack filled with small OBJECTS symbolizing a FOCUS for consideration that can be passed around or back and forth among team members. For example - pull out the small mirror and ask, "What did you see about yourself? What did you see reflected in others?" There are 24 processing sparkers. Call 405-743-2733.

Call **Kendall/Hunt** for their Education/Experiential Science Catalog and Karl Rohnke's books. 800-228-0810

Call **Project Adventure** for a product/publication catalog. 800-796-9917

Jim Cain & Berry Jolliff's book **Teamwork & Teamplay** is filled with more resources than you could ever use. I highly recommend it! Call Kendall/Hunt (the number is above).

EXPERIENTIAL/ADVENTURE-BASED TRAINING COMPANIES

The companies listed here can provide staff training in the Experiential process. I have noted which companies can provide training at your site and which companies provide training in a workshop setting throughout the country.

Chris Cavert
888-638-6565 or Email: chris@fundoing.com
Trainings provided at your site for:
E.A.G.E.R. Curriculum,
Games (and other stuff) for Group, Book 1
Games (and other stuff) for Group, Book 2
Affordable Portables
Games (and other stuff) for Teachers, Book 1
50 Ways to Use Your Noodle
To order books, call Wood 'N' Barnes Publishing & Distribution, 800-678-0621

Leahy & Associates, Inc.
1052 Artemis Circle, Lafayette, CO 80026, 303-673-9832
Adventure Based Training, Challenge Course Building & Development,
Challenge Facilitator Training, Risk Management & Operations.

Learning Unlimited Corporation
5155 East 51st, Suite 108, Tulsa, OK 74135, 888-622-4203 (toll free)
Trainings provided on site and some
workshops in selected areas. Call for schedule.
www.learningunlimited.com

Teamplay
468 Salmon Creek Rd., Brockport, NY 14420
Jim Cain, 716-637-0328

Training Wheels
Michelle McMullen Cummings
1612 Parkside Circle, Layfayette, CO 80026
Training and Portable Game Kits on wheels
www.training-wheels.com

Project Adventure
P.O. Box 100, Hamilton, MA 01936
508-468-7981
Trainings provided in workshop format
throughout the country. Call for schedule.

Leahy & Associates, Inc.
1052 Artemis Circle, Lafayette, CO 80026
303-673-9832

Project Adventure, Inc.
P.O. Box 100, Hamilton, MA 01936
508-468-7981
Equipment Catalog Available

Alpine Towers
Self-Standing Ropes Courses
Mike Feschesser
P.O. Box 69, Jonas Ridge, NC 28642
704-733-0953

Starlight Outdoor Education
Tony Stewart - Equipment Catalog Sales
P.O. Box 96, Smoot, WV 24977
304-392-6306 · 800-845-5692

Course Services
P.O. Box 594, Manchester, PA 17345
717-266-3805

Cradlerock Outdoor Network, Inc.
P.O. Box 1431, Princeton, NJ 08542
609-924-2919

Challenge Masters Associates
Gil A. Chapa
821 Dock St., Box 1-16, Tacoma, WA 98402
206-279-0052 · 800-673-0911
Internet: 102047.2345@compuserve.com
Portable challenge program equiment and training.

Gopher Sport
Sports equipment and portable elements
800-533-0446
(They sell Noodles - Wacky Noodle)

Palos Sports
800-233-5484
(They sell Foam Noodles)

BSN Sports
Sports equipment and indoor climbing walls for schools
800-527-7510

Sportime
800-283-5700

Flaghouse
914-699-1900 · 800-221-5185

Mark One
Sports equipment
800-869-9058

Great Lakes Sports
800-446-2114

REI
The best I can do is the Dallas Number - I'm sure they can get you a catalog.
972-490-5989 or on-line: www.rei.com
(bungee cord resource)

MindWare
Lateral thinking resources
800-999-0398

The Double Balloon

For a stronger long lasting balloon: Using the eraser end of a pencil inserted into a balloon, push the balloon into the inside of a second balloon. Once this is accomplished, blow up the inside balloon (not easy). Tie off the inside balloon and then the outside balloon. (William M. Hazel's "Win Win" Newsletter. Center for Active Education. Vol. 3 Aut. '95.)

The Covered Balloon

For a stronger balloon: Cover the balloon (deflated) with a piece of pantyhose, with one of the ends closed and the other open (on the hose). Blow up the balloon, tie it off, then tie the hose off (William Hazel again).

Ballooshie

For this squishy balloon ball you'll need a small funnel (that will fit into the balloon hole), some flour, and balloons (I have used the 12" size, but the bigger the better). Blow up the balloon to stretch it out - don't tie it off yet. Let the air out. Place the funnel into the balloon and then spoon in the flour. Fill the balloon to your desired size.

Packing the flour creates a harder Ballooshie. Keeping a little air in it gives it a little bounce. If you tie the knot low enough on the neck of the balloon, you can pull the opening back over the floured part to create a rounder and firmer Ballooshie. Experiment with this process to find the Ballooshie that works best for you. (I've even tried Lentils inside a balloon - interesting.)

Tubees

Take an empty aluminum can and cut out the top, the end with the pop-top (picture the can standing upright and cut down along the inside well of the can). The best way to date is using a sharp lock blade knife and with a series of controlled stabbing and sawing motions, zip off the top of the can. Karl recommends wearing gloves to protect against getting cut by the jagged edges. Press the edges flat with a screwdriver.

With the same knife or kitchen shears, cut off the bottom of the can about 1/4" from the bottom. Flatten out the jagged edges. Use some duct tape to cover the edge you just cut.

The throw is like a football pass. Throw with the top forward (the first end you cut out). With practice it should spin and float through the air for a good distance.

Since this activity was written, I have noticed that aluminum cans have become much thinner. Take extra care during the cutting phase not to "squish" the can. (Karl Rohnke's, "Bag of Tricks" Newsletter, #50.)

Websters
Here's a way to use up that old webbing. Cut the webbing into 12" sections (or any other size that will work best for your purpose). Tie an overhand knot at each end of the webbing - as close to the end as possible without the knot loosening out. You have a Webster. These can be used in those hand-holding games that may cause wrist wringer injuries.

UFB (unidentified flying bandanna)
Tie one overhand knot into each corner of your bandanna - about 3" from the tip of the corner. Toss it like a Frisbee. It doesn't fly far, but it has a great parachute effect. I use these UFBs to play a "horseshoes" type of game out on the trail (just push a stick into the ground). What else can you do with a UFB?

B.U.N.
Lay a bandanna flat. Take the two corners diagonal from each other and tie an overhand knot. Do not pull the knot tight, just pull it enough to draw the cloth in together. Take the other corners and tie a granny or square knot (two overhands). This time, pull the knot down a bit tighter to form a ball shape or BUN. You can tuck the corners into the BUN or leave them out for tail. Now you have a soft throwing object for those toss and tag games (or any other game you can think of). It flies pretty well and doesn't roll away after it hits the ground. It's also easy to make, so the group members can form their own ball before playing one of those throwing games. Participatory Gaming!

FLOX
Take one of those cardboard, computer disk boxes - the 3" x 3" style. Be sure to use all the discs first. Fill the box with something of interest. I've used crunched up paper, packing foam (Styrofoam), beans, and rocks. Then tape up the box with some duct tape. You have a **FL**ing-b**OX**. (I do love flying things.) Toss it like a Frisbee. I do have to say that the rock variation turned out to be a little HARD so I don't use this one. But the others are fun. I also like to use different colored duct tape for different FLOXES. SO what can you do with them? Whatever. Just tossing around a box seems to have an interesting appeal. Use it in some games instead of a ball. WHATEVER!

THE TRASH BALL

I am so excited to share this ~~~~~~~~~~~~~~~~~~~ s in PA at the '95 NCCPS #3 ready to learn new things. I didn't have to wait long for "Barnstormin" Bill (William M. Hazel) to show up. And what did he have but, TRASH BALLS! If you always wanted to know what to do with old bags and newspapers (besides throwing them away or recycling them to others) here's a way to use them up. Check the cross section of this marvelous apparatus (see diagram below). These trash or-bitals can be made to any size and hardness. Jeff Wright and I sat on my kitchen floor experimenting. Jeff made a solid one (wrapped very tight–he's got big muscles). This type is good for tossing and catching games–even kicking I would guess. Me, I wrapped a loose one (had nothing to do with the size of my muscles, Jeff, I made another one.) This type is good for "tossing" nicely at others in those tossing-tagging games. Bill recommends sitting down with your group and doing a "facilitated build" (Tom Leahy, 1995), so you can obtain a bunch of trashers without getting your hands full of black ink. Don't you just love Experiential Education!

masking tape - as much as needed.

plastic grocery bag around the outside.

news-paper. Wrapped tight or loose.

paper grocery bag or "Styra" pieces.

ADDITIONAL EQUIPMENT IDEAS:

Submit your additional equipment ideas for possible inclusion in one of Chris' future books to:
Mony Cunningham, Wood 'N' Barnes Publishing, 2717 NW 50th, OKC, OK 73112

174